LOVE'S REVOLUTION

Reimagining Society Through Care and Compassion

A Call to Transform Societal Norms with the Power of Love

CONELL M LOGGENBERG

Table Of Contents

Introduction

This book is aimed at highlighting and addressing the impact of a few inadequately challenged contemporary societal beliefs and practices adversely impacting society, provoking critical thought and stimulating rational discussion towards constructive and meaningful human relations.

Cancelling harmful practices requires the support and active involvement of those affected. However, apathy amongst the affected, much of which is induced by external authorities and those internalised by irrational fear, creates a dilemma amongst the concerned — whether to pursue time-consuming effort for the liberty of others or simply carry on fending for oneself. Torch-bearers against injustice, poverty and harm either dedicate themselves to the cause or conform to the beliefs and practices of a well-oiled socio-economic-political machinery that repeatedly offers platitudes and hollow encouragement to a neighbour struggling under the weight of circumstances not conducive for dignified human existence.

Many people are in need of support and guidance to navigate a meaningful and pleasant existence, but for increasingly low financial earnings coupled with long working hours up against an increased cost of living, motivation and time to effectively address social issues can easily deplete.

These are some of the ingredients of the growing evils which has become the norm, debilitating people's resolve to act decisively against destructive factors. Challenging these factors remains largely the reserve of individuals whose voices remain suppressed by mechanisms such as corporate media shaping public opinion.

Some people, with the luxury of time and money, spend their resources on personal entertainment and gratification of insatiable egocentric activities deemed more important as opposed to alleviating the suffering of others. Commercial-oriented propaganda advances the notion that an individual's suffering is entirely unconnected to anything we do as a collective society.

What this book aims to achieve is to generate awareness that we do affect each other in more ways than we may know or are led to believe. The ultimate objective is to stimulate society into directing its activities, emphasising care for one another. When activities of care dominate society's orientation, its activities for daily living would be reflected as such. The need for the writing of this book does not suggest that care is entirely absent in our society but that care for people is not the dominant or pervasive directive feature driving of our current social order.

Our engagements are directed by commercial activity which manufactures the deprivations at the root of the perpetual state of want a growing number of people unnecessarily find themselves trapped in. A deeper understanding of love and care for our neighbour needs to be cultivated. Love needs to be elevated in our conscience and taught as a subject of supreme importance, over and above any other subject matter. The consequences of actions motivated by love and care for our fellow men/women will undoubtedly make for a better existence for all of mankind.

The current social order is riddled with activity misleadingly construed as already being loving. But with closer inspection, one finds no less rationalisation that upholds a "self love" characteristic of selfishness. This is perpetuated by "powerful" influence perceived as reliable, largely attributed to wider ignorance and unquestioning acceptance of such norms.

Chapter 1

Childhood

During childhood, I had many questions which neither my parents nor my friends had satisfactory answers to, if any at all. As a result, my ongoing life experiences and observation of people's behaviours became my exploration and discoveries about the social order. Like many of my childhood friends, I grew up in a house without electricity; the taps were outside, and the toilet was right back in the furthest corner of the backyard. Toilet paper was old newspaper we had to soften up for wiping ourselves. It was quite common.

Some of the more distinct observations about life and society I made as a child emanates from experiences that have undoubtedly impacted my memory and shaped my view on life.

My mum and dad didn't marry each other, and as a result, I have lived in many homes. My great-grandmother told me that I was 6-months old when I was first left in her care. She went on to tell me that my mum and dad had an argument about whether to stay in the rural area or move to the city.

My dad wanted to stay in Beaufort West, whereas my mum wanted them to move to Johannesburg (today known as

Gauteng, SA). They couldn't agree, and my dad wouldn't allow my mum to take me to Jo'burg. Arrangements amounted to my great-grandmother, my granddad and my grandmother taking custody of me. I don't know how long I've lived with them before moving back to my mum in Port Elizabeth.

One of my earliest memories was that of growing up in Kwanobuhle, a suburb in Port Elizabeth, where, from my childhood memory, very poor people lived. People spoke mainly Xhosa and I had to learn the language. It was the occasional shack, and then, on another day, I'd find myself sleeping on the floor in a house amongst my many cousins. The house was a one-bedroom semi-detached. The lounge & kitchen were makeshift in the same room with a cast iron stove in the corner, and the only bedroom in the house was separated by a curtain in an open doorway. The bedroom was reserved for the elderly, whilst an uncle and aunt shared the lounge floor with my cousins and I. That made five of us in the lounge and an often unknown number of people in the bedroom.

Some of the people sleeping over you'd only get to meet in the evening, whilst others come in late and leave very early the next morning. The bitter smell of grown-up's sweat and smelly socks was slightly repelled by the aroma of sunlight soap. This concoction customarily filled the morning air in the house.

As a child, I had a sense of suppressed rebellion for what I felt wasn't quite fair. The circumstances I saw around me seemed like the norm - a norm I didn't like but didn't know how to address it. It felt like an order I was expected to accept and grow into without question.

It wasn't until my mum got our own house in Uitenhage that I had my own bedroom. It made a big impression on me. I felt special, and a sense of love and care bestowed upon me. I didn't know why, but that's what it felt like until my mum started making demands and giving me a hiding for not having done things I didn't know I was supposed to do. It felt like I always had to please her just to have the privilege of the sanctity of my bedroom, the toys or the food I ate.

The feeling of being loved and cared about quickly dissolved and was replaced with a sense of fear and uncertainty. My mum beat me so many times I had, at one point, actually doubted whether she was my real mum. For a moment, I actually entertained the fantasy that someday I'll meet my real parents.

I remember one night, my mum had a few friends over. They sat in the lounge drinking beer, smoking cigarettes and, despite sitting close to each other, talking very loud. I can't remember what time it was, but I know it was very late at night as I kept nodding off. Each time I had nodded off, my mum would abruptly wake me up, shouting over my head, reminding me to stay awake until they had finished partying. My bedroom was right next to the lounge so it was a short trip for my mum to just pop in.

Eventually, as usual, their partying came to an end with an argument. What it was about, I have no idea. I remember my mum wanting to give me a hiding that very moment for not staying awake throughout the duration of their party. It felt as if like I was to blame for their argument. What saved me was a male guest who intervened and stopped my mum from carrying out her threat.

That was my cue to get ready for the cleanup. I cleared the brown beer bottles, —which I remember bore a red label with the words "Black Label"— odorous beer glasses and emptied all the ash-trays. Then, I had to clean up the beer spillages from the settees and the floor. The settees were easy to clean due to the hard plastic cover on them.

Only after my mum had settled in bed was I allowed to go to bed.

The next morning, I was subjected to the beating my mum couldn't succeed in doing the previous night. I even had to fetch the belt, take it to her and then, of course, take the beating.

School was weird. I'd get up in the morning, get dressed in my school uniform— grey shorts and a blue shirt, grey knee-high long socks and black shoes called "batas"— and take the bus along with other children. My mum would give me twenty cents each day. Ten cents for the bus journey each way.

I remember the different types of buses.

Sometimes, I'd be taking the single deck and other days, it would be a double-decker bus. The double-decker always made me feel good because I could sit on the upper deck from where I could view my surroundings from a different perspective. The same things just seemed so much different from up there. It felt like an escape and gave me a sense of freedom. It also made me hope, think and feel that a different world was possible.

For some reason, the same journey to school felt so much shorter, and I remember feeling a little disappointed arriving so soon at my stop when what I really wanted was for the journey to continue, just anywhere but school.

Only thing I remember about that school was playtime and when a Coca-Cola truck came to deliver free drinks. We could choose between a Coke or a Fanta, served in a small class bottle. This was one of the very few days I was glad to be at school.

On one of my many train journeys with my mum, I remember standing at and holding onto the pane of a half-open train window opposite the second-class compartment we were travelling in. Whilst enjoying the different sounds of the train, the wind and the sight of passing trees, I made a huge discovery - my mum told me it was my birthday.

I had no idea. I didn't know I had one.

I remember turning my head, slightly frowning in amazement, and my eyes looking for answers to a question I couldn't articulate. All I could muster was "oh," smiling, and that was it.

I was 7 years old that day.

I gained a new awareness of myself. A sense of a whole new world I didn't know existed.

Beaufort West:

My mum left for Jo'burg, and I stayed behind with my great-grandmother, grandmother and grandad in Beaufort West. It was a two-bedroom house. My grandad and grandma slept in the front bedroom. I shared the rear bedroom with my great-grandma, my aunt and my uncle.

Here, everyone spoke Afrikaans.

My great-grandma took me to school for enrolment. I remember the school was already in session and I sat in a waiting area whilst she was in an office speaking to the headmaster, a very tall man, Mr Duimpies.

My family in Beaufort West weren't exactly well off, so food was scarce. Something I accepted to be the norm. However, at school, I noted that some of the children had a packed lunch for school. They had white bread with luncheon meat, which we called 'pelony,' and cheese. What's more, is that they even had butter on their sandwiches as well.

One of my school friends lived in the "lokasie," which was an area reserved for people of black ethnicity. He had it far worse than me. He was barefoot often hungry, and we'd maximise playtime because we lived a huge distance from each other. Again, a situation I didn't understand much, but I felt it wasn't right.

Chapter 2

Social Graduation

Our societal system is set up to process us through little stations, which, if we pass through successfully, we arrive at what is considered the seals of what constitutes a successful life. The societal passage for perceived successful progression runs through school, higher education, work, marriage, children and ultimately, retirement before death.

Of all these stages, I shall only make reference to that of school for the purpose of context.

Depending on which part of the world you're in, schooling starts at a very young age, as low as 4 years of age. The impact of this socialisation is varied and has varied outcomes dependent on the family, the school and the community where the child lives and attends school. The child is very much in need of parental supervision, particularly that of his/her parents. Children's emotional needs fulfilment is critical for their development. They need to feel safe in any environment to aid their transition into later independence from their parents.

The realities of socio-economic conditions leave much to be desired, and the conditions are not an accident — they are manufactured.

Housing and schooling differ for children dependent on their parent's financial status. Families with access to vast sums of money benefit their children with comfortable shelter and other basic necessities for the fulfilment of their physiological needs. Money wealth, however, does not guarantee the child's emotional fulfilment from its parents. The dynamics vary greatly.

Desirable, is a family who spends a lot of time with their young children by not only being in their presence, but more so being emotionally present. Money and wealth can afford a family all the luxuries money can buy. These luxury items are, in many cases, contributing to the emotional distance family members may already experience. In others, they become the catalyst for new emotional distance.

One such example is that of television and mobile devices such as phones, computers and online gaming, which connects individuals to a virtual world diverting attention away from people in their immediate vicinity.

Where parents do not enjoy a good relationship, they themselves may find escape in these mechanisms to satisfy their own needs for connection with people. The child often suffers emotional deprivation as a direct consequence of the parents themselves not having emotional fulfilment and thus not having the necessary capacity to attend to the child's emotional needs. Children who growing up in abject poverty where parents do not have access to enough money suffer deprivation in the fulfilment of their physiological needs and, quite often, the double blow of emotional deprivation that could flow out of it.

Children living under poor economic conditions do not automatically suffer emotional deprivation from their parents. Some parents are actually quite rational and resilient about the socio-economic conditions and prioritise their children's needs under the strain. Whilst such parents may be coping very well and giving their children the emotional fulfilment they need, the same cannot be said about all households and the children living under similar conditions.

My childhood friend Stibo[1] grew up in a household where there was no shortage of anything needed to fulfil his physiological needs. Their house was in the middle-class area, fully electrified, complete with a television, and they even had a fridge. The toilet and taps were all inside their house, and they had a bathroom. He had his own bedroom. What's more, is that he could open the fridge at anytime and just help himself to whatever was in it. I saw Stibo taking out the milk from their fridge and drinking the milk straight from the bottle. That was a jaw-dropping moment for my observation. Still remember it to this day. From the perspective of my household and living conditions, you had to be rich to do that.

In my household, milk was a luxury we saw once a month and was not for our household's benefit, let alone the children. It was purchased to compliment the tea and coffee of the church members who gathered at our house once a month for a prayer meeting. I could always count on my great-grandmother's leftovers to have a taste of milk coffee —

---

[1] Nickname for my childhoood friend

and the excess sugar that didn't dissolve at the bottom of my grandmother's cup. I always suspected they used these monthly gatherings as a means to indulge themselves a little because we couldn't really afford to waste sugar like that.

Stibo had a bank account. It even had money in it. At the age of 10, he already had an identity book, much like a passport for domestic purposes. Not that I knew much about it because I didn't know one needed such things. It was all foreign and rich people's privileges, which, in my childhood view, didn't apply to me. A bank account was a symbol of status, which was way out of my league. No one in our household had a bank account. For a child to have a bank account was for me, unthinkable and only implied wealth.

On Sundays, Stibo's mum would cook a delicious meal. The meal would comprise several types of meat — chicken, beef, lamb, pork and turkey. There'd also be roast potatoes, pumpkin, sweet potatoes, corn on the cob and rice. To top it all off, the pudding was canned guava and peach fruit with custard. Sundays were a special bit of heaven. I know of these luxuries because Stibo would ask his mum to let me stay over every weekend. We were like brothers; particularly on Sundays, we were almost inseparable as the fun times grew to a close.

They had a car, and he would insist on me being driven home so that we could have a few more moments together in the car. It was quite a luxury being driven right up to the gate of where I lived. I remember the expression of honour on my grandparent's faces to have a car stopping at ours. The honour and pride were enhanced when Stibo's mum would get out of the car and walk in through our gate to greet my grandparents. For my family, it was a visibly indelible mark of honour and status because the whole street would bear witness to the arrival of a car, stopping at ours and people of middle-class affluence gracing my family with their presence, a handshake and conversation. It was brief, but for my family it was long enough to broadcast a statement of wealth connection.

In the winter evenings, Stibo and I had the task of starting a fire in the cast iron stove to warm up the house and boil water for his mum's tea. They had an electric heater, which was mainly used for short periods of time. We would always make his mum a cup of tea upon her arrival from work, and she would often reward us with chocolates and crisps for having looked after the house while she was at work.

At around the age of 12, Stibo started simulating smoking. He'd take half-burned wood splinters from the fire, hold them between his fingers, suck on them as if it was a cigarette and blow out smoke. Where he had seen this can only be from other people in public because his mum was not a smoker. This became a regular routine of Stibo's whenever we would start the fire. We usually used the finer splintered wood for starting the fire, but he would keep aside some of the splinters for him to light and simulate smoking.

One evening, to my surprise, Stibo took out from his pocket a cigarette butt and lit it at the stove. He had picked it up in the street on our way back from the local café. It became a regular feature of our journey to the café that he would search along the road for discarded cigarette butts. He always got lucky and collected quite a few. He later figured to collect the remaining tobacco from the many butts into a small piece of newspaper which he rolled into what he called a "zol" and smoked it. In the beginning he coughed a lot, but later became quite skilled at it.

Stibo started buying loose cigarettes with the change he kept from the money his mum left for us to buy bread and milk. I had, on many occasions, asked him not to do it. If his mum found out, we'd both be in trouble. He wasn't too concerned because he knew his mum finished work at 7 pm and would usually arrive home at around 7:30 pm. He made sure to do his smoking at around 6 pm when we usually started the fire. That allowed time for the smoke from the fire to overpower the smell of the cigarette smoke.

One fateful evening when had just started the fire, Stibo was still smoking a cigarette when the sound of his mum's car arriving and parking near the kitchen door suddenly filled the air. His mum's early arrival was unexpected. The sound of his mum's car arriving used to fill us with excitement because she'd always bring us something nice to nibble on. Not this time.

The silence that followed the turning off of the car's ignition caused us to scramble like never before. Stibo threw the remainder of the cigarette in the fire and frantically waved his hands in a desperate attempt to eliminate the smell of cigarette smoke that hung thick in the air. Customarily, we would have his mum's tea cup ready with teabag on the table, the boiled water ready for just pouring and one of us would open the door to welcome her back home. This time, we were not ready.

His mum had parked the car right next to the kitchen door instead of the usual space further to the backyard. That made her transition from the car to the kitchen door a very short one. She walked in on us. The smell of cigarette smoke was thick. The look on everyone's faces said it all.

His mum demanded an explanation. I stood there listening as Stibo told a badly constructed lie. His mum didn't buy it. She turned to me. I was left to tell her the whole story. It was clear on her face that neither the lie nor the truth made any difference. She was most disappointed that this was happening.

She sent us packing that very same evening.

We had to pack all our clothes in plastic bags and leave. She was very upset. Stibo was not even allowed to take any of the nice Adidas sports bags to put his clothes in. That evening, we walked to a very deprived area of our town. Stibo led the way. We turned up at a house where a woman welcomed us in without any question.

It was Stibo's biological mother.

He had been an adopted child living with all the luxury I thought he was born into. What a shocker.

Everything at his biological mum's place was the complete opposite of circumstances. The house was a three-roomed semi-detach. Not three bedrooms. Four people were already living there. We have now made it six. The toilet was outside. No bathroom. No electricity. The tap was outside. The furniture was dilapidated. No fridge. The house wasn't clean. There was the smell of sunlight soap, a tinge of shoe polish and body odour that filled the air. I remember seeing a can of Brut men's deodorant as well as a small bottle of Mum roll-on deodorant in what seemed like a proud display. Both deodorant containers were empty. They only served as decoration — more like a statement to convey identification with something other than the obvious reality. There was a visible lack of food.

I stayed there for a few days, not going home for fear of having to explain what had happened.

Stibo soon started smoking dagga (marijuana). It wasn't long before he was introduced to mandrax, a pill that was crushed and mixed with dagga for smoking. The effects on him were unmistakably evident. When he had smoked these drugs, he had a remarkable look of complete relaxedness about himself. He had this perpetual smile for no reason apparent to me. He looked somewhat extra cool and exhibited confidence, enhancing his already very good looks.

All I knew was that Stibo was slipping into a routine that got me worried, but I felt absolutely powerless to intervene.

I went to live with other relatives of mine and continued schooling. The circumstances there were no different than that of where Stibo lived with his biological mum. I got used to it.

Stibo stopped going to school. Over the course of the years that I saw him, there was a remarkable deterioration in him, and he seemed somewhat older than he really was. What I do remember, is that he exhibited this sense of desperate want for anything he could lay his hands on. He later returned to live with his adoptive mum but got kicked out again for stealing and selling items to support his drug habit. I had since finished school higher education and moved abroad. Upon my first holiday back to South Africa, I was shocked and saddened to see the state of him. He was unkempt.

Not the Stibo I knew. He used to be very proud of his appearance. It really saddened me to see the look of low self-esteem in his eyes when we met again after all the many years. When I visited his adoptive mum, he happened to be there on the day. So was his adoptive dad, who had since separated from his adoptive mum. I recall his adoptive mum making a statement comparing his life outcomes to mine, saying that he made all the wrong choices. It was a harsh moral judgement echoed by his then adoptive dad, which I saw cutting Stibo really deep in that moment. His adoptive parents hadn't thought that comment through. It was a relatively common way in which some people of Christian religious conviction spoke to draw moral distinctions regardless of how it may cause others to feel.

I desperately tried to mitigate the awkwardness of the moment. I could see the pain in Stibo's eyes, which even his handsome smile couldn't conceal.

A few days later, I drove up a street in the poorer end of our town. I saw Stibo walking down the street. I stopped the car to greet him. I couldn't tell what he had, but he was high. He said, "Ek kannie glo jy stop vir my nie, my broetjie" ("I can't believe you're stopping for me, my brother"). I replied saying, "Maar natuurlik, jy's my broer en jy sal altyd wees" ("Of course, you're still my brother, and you'll always be")

I told him to get into the car and gave him a lift to where he was going. I could see the appreciation and sense of pride on his face when other people witnessed him getting out of the front seat of a nice-looking car (a rental for my holiday).

A few weeks later, I left to go back abroad.

A few months later, I received a call from a police officer to inform me that he was at a murder scene and that he had awful news. I naturally asked why he was calling me.

Stibo was stabbed to death.

It hurts to think about him. In hindsight, I believe he had suffered emotional deprivation in his life. It made him vulnerable to what he had succumbed to.

The underlying driving factors were socio-economic conditions, which had put pressure on his family to put him up for adoption.

Everybody needs to have their basic needs fulfilled. Both physiological and psychological.

The money-controlled world places huge unnatural pressure on people. It causes people to have to choose between necessities for living. The economic sustainability assertions propagated through higher education, backed by corporate interests and rubber-stamped by governments around the world, are undermining human integrity.

The body count is increasing.

The necessity of a nurturing environment for the safe development of children cannot be overstated.

Chapter 3

Innocence and Ignorance

Growing up in the midst of a society where wealth is on display but out of one's reach is baffling to the untrained mind. With so much going on and so little explained, the societal outcomes we see today have roots in activities we adopt and participate in without critical inquiry.

As children, we are introduced to the world around us through play and lessons. We play with those within the vicinity of our home, and later with others we encounter in organised settings such as pre-school. Play is an important engagement in one's early development. It helps us formulate relationships and agreements with others.

Interesting about pre-school play, is how grown-ups would intervene to ensure children follow a particular set of rules. One such rule is that of sharing. When children are in a tug of war-over the same toy, the grown-up's response is to intervene. The primary reason for intervention is to stop the "war," and the secondary reason is to reiterate the rules of engagement.

The common theme for engagement, instilled into children by parents, is to share and cooperate for the equal benefit of the same items sought after. That principle is reinforced in formal school settings by teachers instructed to watch children play to ensure the rules of engagement are adhered to, and no one is harmed.

At school and other settings such as Church, we are taught to share, cooperate with one another and obey the rules. Yet, in the same breath, we are drawn into competitive activity and told that it's not about winning and that participation is most important. More so, at the end of such activity is issuing awards for performance or achievement deemed better than others. Contrary to common sense is the expectation that those not awarded should just magically be ok.

One can't be blamed for assuming that such rules of engagement or lessons laid down for children at school and Church are reflecting of principles the adult-world lives by. The reality is a narrative pregnant with contradictions and the social outcomes synonymous with bipolar mood disorders and severe dementia.

Bipolar mood disorder is a mental health condition that causes extreme mood swings. Dementia is a term used to describe a group of symptoms affecting memory, thinking and social abilities.

Here's a little story about my Christmas discovery.

The first time I heard about Father Christmas was when my childhood friend, Goliath, told me about him. I was about 7 years old, and it was the day before Christmas. I had no idea how Christmas worked. Goliath told me the secret.

He told me to hang a plastic bag up against the bedroom wall, go to bed early that night and that I must sleep right through the night. He went on to say that while I'd be sleeping, Father Christmas would come. He has a list of all the children who were good children, and he gives them presents. So, he said, in the morning there will be presents in the bag. Everybody knows it, he said. That was breaking news to me.

I took his advice and hastily searched for a plastic bag. I found a yellow plastic bag with a faded marking that read "Shoprite" (a Supermarket in South Africa). There was already a nail in the wall of the bedroom I shared with my great-grandmother, and I hung my bag there. She looked on with a sense of acknowledgement that it was my bag and I then went to bed. It was difficult to fall asleep at first, but I eventually did.

The next morning, the first thing I did was to look straight at the wall where I hung the plastic bag. It was still there, and to my surprise, it looked like there was something in the bag. I could not believe my eyes. It actually worked. The bag had presents in it — four small toy cars, a cowboy gun set and a string of ten red "stokkie-lekkers" (lolly-pop sweets). It worked just like my friend said it would. I was so overwhelmed, and I wanted to thank my friend for sharing this fantastic secret with me. So I ran outside, out of the gate and made my way along the fence in the direction of his house to go and tell him the good news.

As I made my way along the fence, my eyes were still fixed on the toys in my hand as I was still in utter amazement and joy about this miracle man called Father Christmas.

As I lifted up my head whilst running towards Goliath's house, I called out his name, and he called out my name with equal excitement. I slowed down, stopped running and started walking slowly towards him.

He had this massive big smile on his face. He was sat in a big yellow toy car, complete with four wheels and a steering wheel. His feet were visible at the bottom of the car. I couldn't believe my eyes! I remember saying, "en die?" (and this?). Goliath excitedly responded, saying Father Christmas gave it to him for Christmas!

At that very moment, I wondered why Father Christmas would do this. Give him a big car and not do the same for me. It just didn't make any sense.

I felt cheated.

I wanted to talk to Father Christmas to understand what's going on here.

Father Christmas, I was told, lives in the North Pole. I didn't know where that was, and they said he only comes around once a year if you are good and only when you are asleep.

I was not impressed.

The notion of Santa Claus and the happily ever after ending of bedtime stories are deeply disturbing presentations of reality. Children as young as four years old in other countries are forced to work long hours for reasons they don't understand.

The adults who intervene when children are in a tug of war over the same thing, teaching them to share, cooperate with one another and follow the rules under a principle of considering each other's well-being, happen to be the very participants in a world where competition is the order of the day. A world where winners take everything and create losers left on society's fringes.

The world of competition for commercial advantage has its patronage in the same adults who teach their children good manners, go to Church and even send their children to Sunday school to learn about the good and kindness of Jesus, only to return and participate in the contrary.

Chapter 4

Misdirected living

We all have needs for our existence.

A title of honour or other achievements in life does not exempt you from basic human needs. Our needs are fulfilled as far as we can sustain ourselves or be cared for by another.

During the period of legitimised slavery, some people were literally chained. A consensus of human thought and action brought about the removal of that social order. The tangible chains had been removed from people. However, despite the legislated ending of that social order, today, alive and active, is an even worse form of slavery — that which chains the mind. Such chains remain disguised and complex for recognition by many gripped by fear.

Ignorance and irrational fear remain overpowering forces, enabling a sleepwalk into what's probably detrimental to safe human existence.

We chase after promises designed to accommodate only a few. Yet we pursue and hail this course of social order as the only way - as if to prove the repeated indisputable adverse outcomes wrong. The gatekeepers of the current societal order promote ignorance about the dangers and advance incredulity as a response.

Many people are metaphorically blind and in a state of paralysis, unable to free themselves from the invisible chains holding them hostage.

The poorly educated particularly lack the articulate response to defend against this festering abstract oppression. Those who can see these chains also see the complexities that trap so many. An attempt at liberating people from these chains has become a battle that risks loss of livelihood. Those brave enough must be willing to make a sacrifice—give up their own comforts.

For many, courage to act is as uncourageous as the hollow gestures of generous statements that only speak of the desirable. A profound sense of human solidarity implies there is no greater love than one who lays down his life for his brothers and sisters or friends. Many people identify with Christianity and all its fair moral intentions, but such have become the very sounding symbols of mere intention to love as opposed to acting on it. Courage to act seems to suffocate under newfound needs and popular justification, which negates problem-solving action.

There is reasonable religious belief that we are all dependent on "God." The narrative is that God provides for all our daily needs. In practical terms, that narrative comes up against a very disturbing reality.

The issue of capitalism.

Capitalism's underlying emphasis is advancing an individual or a group's economic and political interests to attain a profiting advantage compared to others. A constant competitive environment is bound to create a small number of winners and many losers. Contemporary society remains hell-bent" on celebrating winners as if the "winners" achieved what they have all by themselves. Losers are left to pick up the pieces and live in the shadows as secondary citizens who supposedly do not deserve the spoils "winner people" go on to enjoy under the current social order determination for "success."

This order has an effect on the psychological health of the masses, who find themselves repeatedly told that they're not good enough. Unless they become like the few winners, their lives are shrouded in misery until such time they do something extraordinary to afford themselves a spot in the tier of "successful" people. "Successful People" are considered those with money means to consume as much of purchasable items as they may wish to. As it is, almost everything required for a healthy and productive existence now carries a price tag.

Despite the kind thoughts towards shared prosperity expressed by a few prominent personalities in society, the will to make the necessary changes fades under the pressure of an overwhelming sense of inadequacy amongst the larger part of society. People are far too busy chasing after basic necessities bogged down by the fear of losing their existing, however pathetic, insufficiently providing jobs than to take a meaningful stand to undo what's actually orchestrating their daily struggle.

Many feel defeated, and the response is consistent with a lack of drive to actively participate in effective measures beyond expressing complaints and support for those more vocally courageous to articulate and organise revolutionary activity. This lack of active participation in effective difference contributes to the perpetuated state of social affairs that sees the continued disproportionate advantage of a few. Capitalists find increasing strength and boldness to reinforce their sense of superiority and right of advantage when depressed people repeatedly go back to their un-liberating activities. This set-up has even created a market for motivational speakers and so-called "life coaches" who quite happily exploit the melancholy amongst the disadvantaged majority.

Desperate for change, people fall for the evidently commercially motivated life coaching and motivational speeches, which basically serve to persuade people into the ring of competition where winners and losers are generated. These can be seen in the phenomena of prosperity preachers who prey on the vulnerability of people who are led to believe in a God who will provide for all their needs if they submit themselves to the unquestioning belief of whatever the preacher says.

In the process, they pay a hefty monetary price, too.

The irony, where they fundamentally preach about caring for one's neighbour, is that people go on to engage in a system which is structurally geared to do the exact opposite.

Current social trends raise many questions with varied answers. The answers produced have their origin in the shape of our mind and understanding. The shape of our mind and understanding is dependent on the diet of information we feed on. A pertinent view on a certain matter may be held as unquestionable truth, whilst another view may unravel an uncomfortable truth many in leadership positions are either ignorant about or prefer to have hidden from public view.

Many pastors and leaders promote a form of love for one's neighbour that is blended with selfishness. They speak of love, but their actions and outcomes are an utter perversion of neighbourly love. It may go to explain why those feeding from such leadership revel in the confusion of what makes for genuine peaceful civil rights and responsibilities. We are so easily drawn to reward, often with complete disregard for our fellow compatriots who go unrewarded. It does not leave much to the imagination as to the next generation in the making.

Masses of people are exposed to trends which enjoy a large following, creating the impression that millions of people can't be wrong. This is how many are led without thinking critically about the trend's real direction or the safety of its promise. Have we become so dependent upon the current way of life that we cannot do without it? Some will tell you that you have a choice and that you can choose your direction and, thus, your destiny. That you have a choice is true in itself. Actual 'space' for the exercising and continuation of your authentic own choice is another matter. Our choices are, in reality, interfered with and limited by proxy. The notion that we ourselves cannot be constructively creative for a better life for all is a misleading one.

The choices we currently operate by are a system of crafted economic-objective options to choose from. So, what's the point of propagating choice when these limits are already in place? We could say that without limits, the choices that some might make could have potentially disastrous implications for themselves and, to an extent, for others. So, what are the choices in life we have today? Are they any different from the choices of people who lived in another era?

Are the choices that we make based on a principle that seeks the distribution of necessities fairly amongst all and not orchestrating that any person suffer detriment? Or is the principle the biased propaganda of a commercial world that operates to sell for maximum profit and exclude those who invariably are not by the means the economic order demands for survival?

The daily reality presents us with an unambiguous clarity of answer. The point we argue in favour of depends on the vested interest we seek to protect or advance.

The evident contradiction of the presumed equality emanating from globalisation is now in full view. Blurred vision remains the condition of many people convinced to run a race in which the finishing line cannot be seen.

A blended version of politics, religion and capitalism continues to sow confusion and conflict over what is more important in life. It mostly propagates the acquisition, accumulation and possession of material wealth as chief activity above anything else. It confuses the religiously virtuous trapped in conflict with their morals, resulting in desperate actions for absolution from moral hypocrisy.

The crafted socio-economic justice system holds us all at ransom. Unexamined euphemisms daily feed society as acceptable guidance. Served up is a main dish of falsehood blended with little truth. We adhere to a blend of moral authority with clearly despicable conduct. There is a strong gut feeling that we are in very bad company.

Chapter 5

Societal Dysfunction

Middle, and lower-class societies experience pressure from two sides of which neither gives them certainty or solution in their quest for security and stability.

Religious faith on the one end and ruthless capitalism on the other. Religious faith drives emphasis of human activity focussed on the equal best interest of our fellow men, whereas capitalism's incentives are rooted in maximising one's own consumption-advantage at the expense of another.

Christianity postulates that one cannot serve both God and Mammon if you serve God.

The New King James Version of the Bible, Luke 16:13 states:

"No servant can serve two masters; for either he will hate the one and love the other, or else he will be loyal to the one and despise the other. You cannot serve God and mammon."[2]

The simultaneous operation of these two opposing principles is the root of hypocrisy, which provides for a talk in favour of one principle whilst actively engaging in the contradictory. When confronted with this reality, cognitive dissonance and irrational argument prop up the indefensible.

---

[2] The New King James Version Luke 16:13

People find themselves persuaded to virtuously pursue salvation stored up in a different life elsewhere whilst turning a blind eye to the induced suffering their neighbour endures in contemporary life's presumed necessary participation in capitalism. Contemporary Christian religious practice can be described as nothing more than moral escapism trapped in a cycle of absolution from "sins" repeated before and after the sermon and prayer. The real impact on the individual is reflected in social conduct and outcomes. It has little to no effective change impact on socio-economic-order reality.

Evangelism is tasked with converting "others" into the fold of the "chosen," typically those who are considered to be on the "wrong" path of salvation. The notion that some are God's chosen people amounts to a pretext for division, entitlement and a superiority complex. The leadership of such doctrine usually enjoys an affluent upper or middle-class lifestyle. Some of their followers may already enjoy the same and simply echo propaganda to stimulate and mobilise the aspirations of the unconverted, who usually comprise an underclass hungry for material "blessing" and salvation.

Material affluence is subtly promoted and rationalised as a blessing from God. It projects an undertone that God loves the wealthy and despises the poor. Therefore, to be in favour with God, the poor are seduced to follow the conduct of the wealthy if they want the "blessing of God." The playing field for manipulation and exploitation couldn't be more obvious. These are the perverted religious messages that promise salvation through slavery instead of love. Where love is concerned, it is directed at personal wealth advantage, as opposed to the simultaneous beneficial outcomes for one's neighbour.

The preacher knows the game all too well. He goes to sleep unbothered in material comfort after another successful session of preying on the insecurities of a people desperate for resources under money control. What these preachers, in covert tones of appealing words, actually proclaim is that the path to heaven is paved with money and not the love for one's neighbour they so loudly talk about. Active Love for their neighbour is either sporadic or nonexistent. Conduct away from the pulpit is the full-blown, unapologetic display of what really matters — the exerting of more energy in a commercialised world to maximise personal consumption whilst paying lip service to the poor and destitute in society.

You don't need to look very far — the Catholic Church, the Church of England, World famous Evangelists like Thomas Dexter Jakes, Joel Osteen or Shepherd Bushiri from Malawi and many other similar self-made preachers. It's purely business wrapped up in packaging that appeals to their follower's insecurities.

Defence of the embarrassing lie is their justified need for another sermon to be absolved of the "sin" they supposedly have no control over. The Church's emphasis on the follower submitting his will to the God they preach about is dangerous ground. The God the Church refers to is the God nobody sees. The belief propagated is that God is ever-present in spirit and reveals himself through his spoken word.

It is further believed that the word of God is to be found in the vessels of such with designated ministry. In other words, God gives the message to the minister, who then reveals it to the followers in the form of a sermon or teaching. The belief that the minister is infused with the spirit of God or has opened himself up to God's spirit is used as grounds to justify whatever the minister says or does as unquestionably the will of God. Questioning the minister's words or doubting anything he says would be as if questioning or doubting God.

This concept has an inherent design for exploitation. It is visible in the relationship we see between the Church and the member who is asked to just have faith. What the member may not realise is that the Church, in its ministers, positions itself as God. Dispute with the Church or the minister is considered going up against God the Almighty. The mere thought of such a stance is to fill the disputing church member or person with fear that God would cause him unbearable suffering in this life and the propagated next.

Obedience is thus considered an imperative virtue if the individual wants salvation.

And so the Church tells the followers that it is God's will that they repent and submit themselves to God because, as the Church has us all believe is that we are all sinful by default and in need of the sacraments from the Church to be saved. What the Church is really saying is to lay down our God-given capacity to think for ourselves and instead accept instruction from the Church, which is exclusively endowed with God's word, which will tell us how to think and ultimately behave. This pious approach should give the rational thinking mind cold chills because the reality presented by the contemporary Church is riddled with inconsistency and contradiction which causes necessary deeper inquiry to reveal underlying motivation.

The "antichrist" we are warned against is comfortably nestled and nurtured amongst us. It also runs governments, banks, food stores, farms, schools, councils and churches. Common sense tells us that actions speak louder than words, but the Church and its pastors have us believe that their words are enough.

Church can serve as a perfect submission of the self to authority. Also, the perfect escape from responsibility.

Many religious-oriented people claim that God or the Spirit inspires them to do what they do. They believe that the direction their lives take couldn't have anything to do with the decisions they make as adults. I reference "adults" because children are very much under the guidance and influence of their parents, teachers and leaders whom they rely on for their nurturing.

Many churches expect adults to behave like children in their relationship with God and the Church - that of being "obedient" and subjecting themselves unquestioning to the propagated doctrine, and to reinforce the same mannerism into their children to ensure they are the perfect subjugated personalities which depend on Church and authority for everything they do or wish to do.

Such individuals always require the permission, approval or "blessing" of the Church or the church minister for whatever they seek to embark upon. The same behavioural expectation often leads to conflicts in relationships where a married man holds the perverted view that his wife should do whatever he says and never question his actions, even if he is abusing her. These perversions play out in people's social relationships, too, because of what they project as unquestionably the will of God.

Take, for example, the attitude of Western governments, who believe themselves to be under God, towards African governments and their people – for example, how the Benjamin Netanyahu-led Israeli government considers the lives of people of Palestinian origin or Arab nations less than that of their own under the auspices of being God's special people.

Church never takes any blame or responsibility for any outcome which serves a believer's disadvantage, but is quick to take credit for that which results in an advantageous outcome for the believing follower. Suppose a believing follower does not have the desired results of an endeavour the Church, and ministers comfortably absolve themselves from any responsibility and refer to the outcomes as a matter of God's will, even though they may have given their "blessing."

This is when the believer quickly realises that responsibility for the adverse outcomes is his to bear. He then seeks to shrug off the responsibility in the same way as the minister so conveniently does, by following a perverted indoctrination that you can simply cast your burdens onto God or Jesus through the Church, and you'll be better for it. It should be noted that this luxury doesn't come without a price — continued submission of the self to Church and minister and at least ten per cent of whatever you earn to cover up your miserable existence.

It isn't until you free yourself from the debilitating mindset that you start experiencing life for what it really is, as opposed to the blindfolds and fantasy of perverted church doctrine.

Reality is that we make decisions about what we do, and the responsibility for outcomes lands upon us as individuals or as a collective. There is also the much-overlooked impact upon us from other people's doing — that of our parents, the Church and its expectations, the pressure exerted upon us by the political and economic system, the constant competition under the illusion that success is high financial earnings and material wealth as opposed to caring and mutually beneficial co-existence with one another.

If God is in charge of everything we do, then there's utterly no point in the ability to exercise thought. We'd be automatons in a game designed with predetermined outcomes because the responsibility isn't ours.

Greed and the killing of people would thus all fall under the responsibility of God, whom the Church claims and propagates as being in control of everything. However, the Church and its ministers enjoy their irrational authority and freedom of playing the dual card game, which perpetuates their subtle sadomasochistic relationship with so-called "sinners." If they were to give it up, they'd have to face reality instead of the perverted moral authority exploitation of people.

Departure from contemporary church control of the mind would set off the freeing of many trapped in the romance of irresponsibility for the effect of their actions. God is not responsible for what we do. We are. It is no wonder that the commercial-oriented mindsets continue to bathe themselves in absolution for the disparity and human suffering caused by their greed-motivated actions they label as entrepreneurism. The same people bear the "blessing" of the Church, who ironically encourage people to strive for material wealth, in that they even pray for it and celebrate it as a "blessing" from God, from which a repeated ten per cent goes to feed the insatiable need of the Church.

Most people today are stifled into a prolonged or permanent state of poverty because everything is already pre-owned, including faith. No wonder the Church presides over an insatiable flock wandering in a perpetual state of want.

As long as the means of production and that deemed necessary for a safe existence remain privatised and under commercial control, we will remain in a vicious circle of endless want and its predictable consequences we have grown so accustomed to.

Where the means of production belong to all and serve all, there would be purposeful activity to produce and issue to all. Churches and their leaders actively contribute to perpetuating the suffering of people by participating in the commercialisation of what's needed to survive. They sell faith and access to heaven in a variety of packaged euphemisms.

The ultimate grip they gain over your conscience is enough to induce guilt if you don't obey them or the wicked masters of the day. They hide behind the sanctity of the gospel, which, if properly applied, is to profit the soul. Instead, they are more intent on helping themselves to the spoils of an ungodly practice. Ever wondered why they're always well dressed, well fed, live in comfortable accommodations, drive expensive cars, can afford healthcare and have retirement provisions? With all these comforts in place, they have no problem encouraging you to do things that make little or no change to your circumstances or the state of social affairs.

If they are at all passionate about fairness, why don't they act against the order of the world? They seem more intent on obeying the daily governments to be deemed "good citizens" rather than addressing injustice against God's creation orchestrated in plain sight.

Jesus sacrificed himself. Church repeatedly reminds people of it. So why reserve the beneficial outcomes of the gospel and Jesus' sacrifice for the soul's end journey?

The soul is here and now, presently suffering under the weakness of the flesh in which it resides. If we are only to focus on the life that awaits us as a reward for enduring injustice, then what's the point of living or participating in this life? If the propagated next life is better than this one, then, for the love of God, why are we wasting this existence suffering injustice?

Is injustice necessary?

Is injustice the path to love and peace?

Is Injustice the path to heaven?

The contemporary Church is not innocent of indulgence in the obscure and invidious system of commercialism that corrupts and condemns people to the hell they experience. It has become a heartless advocate for the very system it inherently should oppose. Instead, it appears to work harder at our destruction, as opposed to our construction, for which Jesus offered himself as the cornerstone.

It must be said that isolating the benefits of Jesus' sacrifice as a reserve for the soul's end journey appears to be the perfect excuse to conduct a rampant unneighbourly existence. After all, Jesus said: Love God above all and your neighbour as yourself.

The irony of contemporary Christian conduct could not be more explicitly embarrassing. It loves the notion of loving God, but the instruction to love our neighbour is clearly an inconvenience. The Church's self-preservation, despite Jesus' sacrifice, is complicit in people's suffering. No wonder the 'devil 'does not bother with the Church. It's perfect.

In the story of the good Samaritan (Bible, Luke 10:25-37), we learn how we ought to relate and help one another. Today, this somewhat happens to an extent. But do we have to wait for someone to suffer before we do anything? Sadly, the story of the good Samaritan does not inspire everyone. Jesus concluded this teaching with: "Go and do likewise."

A commercial environment is the breeding ground for selfishness, and makes a mockery of the contingency for

Samaritan conduct. The underlying strength of social problems is the connective tissue made of money.

Churches preach to people to be charitable and to use their talents to advance God's work, except the government of the day.

If the government of the day is not the administrative authority of The Good Lord, then who are they?

Although Church and state are operationally separated, their underlying code of conduct is laced with menace towards anyone who disagrees with operations that clearly engage people as a means to an end for the benefit of a "qualifying" few. The individual does not dare to challenge the organisation's menace for fear of not being "loved" by the organisation. Organisations prescribe what and how individuals are to be and only engage them on the conditions they set. It is thus required of the individual to be anything but themselves — the individual is required to acquire "qualifications" if he is to be accepted as a useful being. No wonder large organisations and corporations rule the day. We have been caged by a mere promise of freedom. We fell for it without due diligence about the affect upon our neighbour.

Love on condition of this, that and the other is what continues to mislead us into the abyss of chaos.

Jesus said: Love God above all... And love your neighbour as yourself. Why do we have so many interpretations of the same statement? Could it be that we only look for an explanation that serves advantages to some and disadvantages to others? That is the very nature of Politics. Not Love.

Politics divide.

Love unites.

God has given us freedom.

God's freedom is also peace to us and full of peace for us... so why, then, isn't it working out in this way?

Somewhere along the line of our lives we have been influenced by suggestions we carelessly followed. Many of us understand this to be the work of evil. Many still stand to disagree, seeking evidence. So good is the disguise of evil that it hides in plain sight. It remains the best trick. Many remain perplexed by the contrast of findings but nonetheless continue under the spell of toxic short-term solutions.

Toxic solutions are those that only hold posture by the strength of money support.

The God we love has become the one we keep in our back pocket for when we need it. A god we can control... So we made one... Money.

The complexity of economic jargon hides the truth about the inevitable destruction it sows in its wake. We are engaged in processes to which we did not invent or provide informed consent. We are operating systems we don't understand. We are ruled by laws we did not make. We are made managers of a social system we did not design.

We are so busy in this system that we don't even realise that the system is actually managing us.

Chapter 6

Usury — The Trap

Buried in the complexity of laws people don't know about or understand is a disturbing design that, if it were to be challenged, the real gangsters who conspire against the people would be revealed by their rebellion. Dislodging and discarding that design would usher in the dawn of the dissolution of the manufactured problems in society.

Usury, a practice referred to in the Old Testament of the Bible (Deuteronomy), is lending money and charging interest on that loan to enrich the lender. Usury remains in practice to this day. The detrimental effect of usury can be demonstrated in a simple game of musical chairs.

As long as the music plays, all chairs are in the game. Every time the music stops, a chair disappears. Start out with 10 players and provide each with a chair. When the music starts, everyone gets up from their chair and starts dancing. One chair is removed before the music stops. When the music stops, one person would be left without a chair to sit on.

Think of the chairs as the supply of money. As long as there's a money supply, people can spend on food and clothes and even pay their mortgages. However, if too much currency is created, it causes inflation of the currency and a rise in the price of goods and services.

The central bank, whose main objective is the protection of the currency from hyperinflation, will thus move to cause a contraction in the currency supply to protect the currency's value. As a result, somewhere, someone in the interdependency of the currency supply will default on their debt obligation and will lose what they had. Similar to not having a chair to sit on.

Bankers and economists, through indoctrinated views that they ensure students at school and universities are made to believe, are keen to dismiss this argument with complex economic jargon. The bottom line is that debt-fuelled commercial activities only lead to casualties in the chain, and their manufactured complexity of smoke and mirrors delivered in euphemism hides this truth. The practice of usury is glorified as good for the progressive development of society under the auspices of 'economic growth.' Despite the repeated destructive outcomes delivered by this practice, people still believe that somehow it won't happen again. This type of belief is synonymous with insanity.

When people are insane, they pose a danger to themselves and or others. And when this is the case, under our Mental Health laws, such persons should be "sectioned" for rehabilitation. The record of history is overwhelmingly compelling evidence that this very practice requires forthwith quarantine if we indeed care about people at all.

The parable in Matthew 25:14-30 tells of a master who was leaving his home to travel and, before going, entrusted his property to his servants (property worth 8 talents, where talent was a large unit of money, as discussed below). One servant receives five talents, the second two talents, and the third one talent, according to their respective abilities.

Returning after a long absence, the master asks his servants for an accounting. The first two servants explain that they have each put their money to work and doubled the value of the property they were entrusted with, and so they are each rewarded.

His Lord said to him, "Well done, good and faithful servant. You have been faithful over a few things. I will set you over many things. Enter into the joy of your Lord."[3]

The third servant, however, has merely hidden his talent in a hole in the ground and is punished:

He also, who had received the one talent, came and said, "Lord, I knew you that you are a hard man, reaping where you did not sow and gathering where you did not scatter. I was afraid and went away and hid your talent in the earth. Behold, you have what is yours."

But his Lord answered him, "You wicked and slothful servant. You knew that I reap where I didn't sow and gather where I didn't scatter. You ought, therefore, to have deposited my money with the bankers, and at my coming, I should have received back my own with interest. Take away, therefore, the talent from him, and give it to him who has the ten talents. For to everyone who has will be given, and he will have abundance, but from him who doesn't have, even that which he has will be taken away. Throw out the unprofitable

---

[3] World English Bible Matthew 25:23

servant into the outer darkness, where there will be weeping and gnashing of teeth."[4]

Such a literal interpretation of this particular text presumes that Jesus approves of the conduct of that master in the parable. It couldn't be further from the truth. An argument which leans towards such an interpretation is more likely to distort Jesus' ethics on brotherly love.

Firstly, the 'Lord' in the parable is not Jesus, and neither should Jesus, given his principles, be insinuated to such literal ends. The "lord" is a title people of wealth and influence bore. The property of the 'lord' in the parable is earthly goods. The parable merely demonstrates a practice which was the order of the day and helps people understand the consequences. Jesus' message is not aimed at earthly gain but spiritual gain, which benefits the soul. See the following quotes from the Bible:

Jesus looked at him and loved him. "One thing you lack," he said. "Go, sell everything you have and give to the poor; you will have treasure in heaven. Then come, follow me."[5]

And also from Matthew:

19"Do not store up for yourselves treasures on earth, where moth and rust destroy, and where thieves break in and steal. 20"But store up for yourselves treasures in heaven, where neither moth nor rust destroys, and where thieves do not

---

[4] Matthew 25:24–30, World English Bible

[5] Mark 10:21

break in or steal; 21 for where your treasure is, there your heart will also be.[6]

What is also clear in the parable is that there is a master and slave relationship where the master simply wants things done regardless of whether someone else's life is at risk. In contrast, Jesus seeks to treat us as equals, and His actions are geared towards rescue (salvation) rather than condemnation and destruction of the individual's 'equitable' condition of his soul. That equity in the soul ought to be translated into our lives here on earth. In the prayer that Jesus taught (Matthew 6:10), it states: 'Thy will be done in earth, as it is in heaven.'

Although Jesus uses the parable of the talents to describe heaven, he makes it abundantly clear that God's pleasing conduct demonstrates care for others — that which does not cause people to lack necessities for their safe existence.

---

[6] Matthew 6:19-21

Chapter 7

Money

Money in contemporary society is what determines people's quality of living. It serves as the means to acquire goods required for existence, apart from oxygen, of course. Money is almost all qualifying means for whatever you may want in this world because everything is up for sale.

It is thus clear that if you didn't have the money you're clearly faced with a hurdle. Despite it being a pervasive aspect of our society, it isn't a subject that is taught with any intensity for critical review about its negative impact on human life, other than being hailed as necessary to balance human motivation and that of the economy. The economy and all its jargon are reserved for the institutionally educated, whose curriculum is designed by the creators of money, ensuring that money remains relevant and unchallenged as to its necessity and impact. Strange is the different types of currency in circulation, of which some are accepted as more valuable than others — typically the currency of Western countries versus that of an African country. For example, the British Pound is worth R24.00 (twenty-four South African Rands). That positions the holder of a British pound to buy 24 times more than anything that is valued at R1.00

What's odd about this setup is that much of what the British and European countries need for their natural existence or for conducting their commercial activities is found in Africa. The arrangement is a blatant disproportionate convenience, which makes it easy for them to buy goods from Africa and live the comfortable lifestyles that they do in comparison to the majority of people living in Africa. Their further proxy control of other basic necessities by way of investment into private companies that run such services ensures the subjugation of many people who do not have access to the money supply. Many are left to work incessantly hard and long hours to earn a low wage and having to pay for necessities priced to exceed their budget.

Debt becomes the noose around the neck of many people who, due to low income, take out loans and having to pay it back with interest. When such loans cannot be paid, they end up losing whatever property they may have had because the institution of bailiffs is the heartless hammer that nails the misery deeper into people's existence. They care not about the impact of their actions other than the money their vile practice brings them and those who instructed them. Their motivation is the same as the person who instructed them — Money. Not to help people.

If money was removed from society, human interactions would be affected differently. The notion that people would be demotivated to do anything is a fabrication that undermines the human spirit to take care of one another motivated by love.

It is the lack of love as well as the lack of belief and practice of love that people turn to money as a regulator for human activity. It is also an expression of people's lack of trust in one another that they'd rather an external force regulate their behaviour as opposed to soliciting the motivation of loving actions from within themselves. It's evident in many people who, despite attending church or even being preachers of religious doctrine that speaks of love, cannot see the irony of their own conduct. They participate in the very system of money that works the misery they hope and pray everyone can be relieved from.

The solution stares them right in the face. Practice Love. Not commerce. To do that, you must discard all forms of money. "No one can serve two masters. Either you will hate the one and love the other, or you will be devoted to the one and despise the other. You cannot serve both God and money."[7]

Also the following is worth a read

18 Once, a religious leader asked Jesus this question: "Good Teacher, what should I do to inherit eternal life?" 19"Why do you call me good?" Jesus asked him. "Only God is truly good. 20But to answer your question, you know the commandments: 'You must not commit adultery. You must not murder. You must not steal. You must not testify falsely. Honor your father and mother." 21 The man replied, "I've obeyed all these commandments since I was young."

---

[7] Matthew 6:24

22When Jesus heard his answer, he said, "There is still one thing you haven't done. Sell all your possessions and give the money to the poor, and you will have treasure in heaven. Then come, follow me." 23But when the man heard this, he became very sad, for he was very rich. 24 When Jesus saw this, he said, "How hard it is for the rich to enter the Kingdom of God! 25 In fact, it is easier for a camel to go through the eye of a needle than for a rich person to enter the Kingdom of God!" 26 Those who heard this said, "Then who in the world can be saved?" 27 He replied, "What is impossible for people is possible with God." 28 Peter said, "We've left our homes to follow you." 29"Yes," Jesus replied, "and I assure you that everyone who has given up house or wife or brothers or parents or children, for the sake of the Kingdom of God, 30 will be repaid many times over in this life, and will have eternal life in the world to come."[8]

---

[8] Luke 18:18-30

Central Bank Digital Currency:

Central banks have now decided to introduce a digital form of money. As commercial trends go, the invention is promoted as a good idea to keep everyone safe from the complications associated with paper money.

These complications range from fake money, transit heists, money laundering and recently, the so-called risk of transmitting disease via notes and coins. This form of money is being promoted for its expediency, instantaneous transaction ability and convenience, but its dangers aren't fully disclosed. The risks and effects on human relations are a subject not included for deliberation by governments who, by the history of their response, had become mere administrators of Central Bankers' Policy instead of taking instruction from the citizenry who's elected them into a role to manage societal affairs for the benefit and safety of all.

The danger of control.

CBDC is precisely the central bank's digital currency and not yours. It means the central bank is in control of it, and you are not. What's worse, and the bankers do not hide it, is that the currency will be programmable. It means that the central bank can issue that currency with specific restrictions, such as what it can be spent on and where and also set an expiration date for it. With such control over currency, the already illusion of freedom and democracy is completely out of the window. People sold by the convenience of CBDC are either in denial or blind to the implications for human rights recorded by the United Nations.[9]

People's rights are hereby effectively being converted from inalienable to programmable. People's behaviour would be dictated by an external authority that overtly threatens to deprive them of fulfilling their existential needs.

The external authorities are an already organised group of people who own and operate central banks around the world through dedicated teams of people desensitised enough to cause human suffering without a second thought just to please their masters. These are people operating large businesses and selling goods in exchange for digital money in their digital accounts, which would also be under the control of and accessible by the central bank. They would be required to only sell to persons with electronic permission to enter their stores and purchase the items their digital money is programmed to purchase.

Take, for example, freedom of speech. If you were to criticise a corporation or a product they had manufactured and sold for public consumption, such as the "covid-vaccines," you could be penalised and have your digital account switched off, and you can't enter a shop, purchase or rent anything.

The currency is designed to be programmable —meaning the bank can determine what and where the currency may be spent.

For example, you may not be allowed to spend currency designated for utility such as gas, electricity or water on food

---

[9] https://www.un.org/en/about-us/universal-declaration-of-human-rights

or for the purpose of travelling. Your freedom of movement would be at risk of being violated in that currency could be programmed to allow its spending only within a specified zone or area determined by the issuing authority. If not the issuing authority, border or zone control agencies could decline payment for travel on instruction from other agencies whom they collaborate with. If, for example, you wanted to board an aircraft to go to another country, your digital payments could be turned off remotely.

The same applies to people who may wish to purchase essentials such as food, but because their currency is remote-controlled, it can simply be suspended or turned off remotely.

This is the perfect setup that Klaus Schwab and his clan at the World Economic Forum seek to achieve — that people own nothing, except those they consider elites because of their money and wealth control over resources — that they can arbitrarily deny you access to anything if you disagreed with anything they do or if you do not comply with their demands. Such happened in Canada in 2022 when the Trudeau-led government imposed irrational restrictions on the movement of Canadians due to COVID. A large number of Canadians objected to the impositions on their freedom and formed a convoy of trucks travelling to the capital in defiance. The Trudeau-led Canadian government retaliated by freezing access to the money raised to fund the effective activities of the resistance. This was a chilling display of power and control where the control to your access to money is simply at the push of a button by an authority you have no control over.

In the New International Version of the Bible, Revelations 13:17, it reads: "so that they could not buy or sell unless they had the mark, which is the name of the beast or the number of its name."

The introduction of CBDC, for many people professing the Christian religion, is considered that very instrument of the mark of the beast. It is considered the means of evil to control people and cause them to behave as dictated. This implies that the notion of democracy would be completely set aside, and governments, like any person or institution, would be under the full control of the central bankers.

It is very clear that those in control of the money and its production are, in fact, a cartel whose product is an unnatural creation serving as a wedge that interferes, obstructs and or destroys natural human relations for a peaceful existence. This leaves the door wide open to the question of whether people would actually be able to regulate themselves without the instrument of money to limit what they can or can't do. What are the alternatives to the human problems central bankers seem to believe money solves?

I return to the point that religions, such as Christianity in its current form, do little to nothing to safeguard people from the "sins" they preach for them to avoid. It is also the case that people depending on the church for their absolution are also misdirected in that they outsource their solutions to an institution that itself is dependent on the product of central bankers (money) instead of the "love of God."

The church instructs its members as per Luke 13:16 (Bible, New International Version): "No one can serve two masters. Either you will hate the one and love the other, or you will be devoted to the one and despise the other. You cannot serve both God and money."— but the church does the exact opposite.

The elaborate answers church administrators and pastors give are a basic form of denial, gaslighting and defending of the indefensible.

Whilst the church can be a wonderful place of gathering in encouraging the best of human relations and behaviour, it is ultimately people's actions that speak much louder after the church gathering. They simply go on to engage in the very money-based rules system they know they should abandon — meaning they serve both God and Money.

What, then, can be done to undo what has seemingly ensnared and corrupted even the church and, thereby, its members?

Money is involved in all aspects of people's lives.

In order to resolve an issue as big as this, deliberate actions need to be taken by groups of people to bring about differences incrementally in small circles and eventually affect the larger community in which those people live.

For this to take effect, it requires the internal adjustment of people first. Not an external rule that drags people into doing something they themselves do not believe in or understand.

Actions motivated by love for our neighbour would have to be an internal motion.

The book of Mark states: "Nothing outside a person can defile them by going into them. Rather, it is what comes out of a person that defiles them."[10]

We hear and see many things around us. We hear and see instances of an evil nature and also things which bear characteristics of neighbourly love. All of these "go into us." Hearing about the beautiful love of God in a church sermon, equally does not automatically make us loving and considerate of our neighbour.

What we do about what we hear, see or know is what ultimately matters. That is what comes "out of us."

In light of all the happenings around us —that which happens to ourselves and to other people—it is for each of us to ask what it is that comes "out of me" that contributes to the environment we find ourselves in.

Am I making matters for myself and my neighbours worse or better? What am I adhering to? What internal principles determine what comes out of me — what is it that I do?

Whilst we may be conditioned by circumstances and the environment we grow up in, we are only in as far as we do not think for ourselves. If purely the environment of external forces directs what we do, we effectively lend ourselves to manipulation, exploitation and control from external forces.

---

[10] Bible, New International Version Mark 7:15

Those external forces, be they good or evil, if we do not ponder on them, we've lost control of ourselves.

Many people love the notion of "giving themselves over" to God, and in doing so, believe that they are now "saved." Inherent in this principle, is also that they don't have to think for themselves, but each time wait on an instruction from God who tells them what to do. This gives credit to the belief that they cannot be held accountable for what they're doing because they're simply doing God's will. Well, the same could be said of someone who "gives themselves over" to any other entity "outside" of themselves. They would thus also have credit to bathe in the defence that it's not them doing what they do, but the entity they had given themselves over to.

We are exposed to many beliefs which amount to "external influence." If we allow for this external influence to "dictate" what comes out of us, we are indeed "only a noisy gong or a clanging cymbal" as per 1 Corinthians 13:1 (Bible, New Living Translation), which reads:

"If I could speak all the languages of the earth and of angels but didn't love others, I would only be a noisy gong or a clanging cymbal."

This manner of response to "external influence" is what renders people vulnerable to the external control of central bankers who already enjoy very little to no resistance from "Christians" to their introduction of Central Bank Digital Currency, a "mark of the beast' to which people, such as "external stimuli dependent Christians," are easy targets for manipulation, exploitation and control under this "beast system" of control.

To statements such as above, often, the Christian mind may seek rebuttal in the statements such as in Proverbs 3:5 to "Trust in the Lord with all your heart and lean not on your own understanding." Or "Be not wise in thine own eyes: Fear the Lord, and depart from evil."[11] It is easy to misunderstand the use of language in these expressions when one is conditioned to the tune of literally experiencing God as an "external" entity and that you are or have no part of God in you. It may go to explain why, in many Christian circles, the words in 1 Corinthians 6:19, which states: "...your bodies are temples of the Holy Spirit, who is in you, whom you have received from God."[12] escapes many for understanding that God is a part of them.

In John it states, "...the Father, the Word and the Holy Ghost: and these three are one."[13]

This implies the same God is in you.

Given our capacity to think, it cannot be the case that, because God is now inside us, our ability to think and make decisions is thereby disabled. If it was the case that God was now fully in control of us, we couldn't possibly do anything unpleasing or contradicting God's will or ways. The spirit in us is "in-fluence." We are also "influenced" by "other spirits."

---

[11] Prov. 3:7

[12] 1 Corinthians 6:19, Bible New International Version

[13] 1 John 5:7

It is thus clear that we possess the ability to decide, and that process takes place "inside" of us, determining what comes "out of us."

Therefore, given what we know from what we are influenced by or informed with, provided that we "think about it," we would be positioned to take responsibility for what we do.

Responsibility means to be in a position of authority over someone or something and to have a duty to make certain that particular things are done. People who believe that God is in charge or in control of their lives typically do not accept responsibility for what happens in their lives. They blame others. They consider that it is God's will that things happen the way they do and that they have absolutely no input or ability to affect anything around them. These are the perfectly subjugated mindsets that people such as central bankers depend on for their manipulation, exploitation and control of people because such people already believe that what's happening is inevitable or fate.

It begs the question of why people afflicted by what they consider unfortunate circumstances or oppression would complain or pray for difference. Shouldn't they just be content with God's decision?

Or why do pastors insist that people pray to God to change the circumstances in their lives or postulate that if people gave monetary offerings to the church, God would look favourably at them? Yet, in the same breath, they cannot hear themselves that if the person afflicted did not pray, the responsibility for the ill-fortunate suddenly becomes their own responsibility.

Another aspect of "responsibility" is that of being able to respond. Children cannot really be held responsible for landing in difficulty when they lack the information or necessary capacity to discern between what's good, bad or safe. Adults, dependent on what they know and discharging their ability to think, could avoid the pitfalls of what's presented to them if they accepted responsibility for themselves. The fear of responsibility is often masked by reference or reliance on Psalm 55, which states: "Give your burdens to the LORD, and he will take care of you. He will not permit the godly to slip and fall."[14] It's easy to see how people could absolve themselves from responsibility when they consider God as an authority "outside" of themselves, despite the same teaching or belief that God lives "inside" them.

Perhaps inadvertently set aside by adult Christian Religion followers is that they forget the admonishment in 1 John, which states: "Dear friends, do not believe every spirit, but test the spirits to see whether they are from God because many false prophets have gone out into the world."[15]

This implies that the believer has to think and take responsibility for what they follow or act upon.

However, as is often the case, many people aren't privy to all relevant information to enable them to make a decision about what they're offered. The lack of knowledge about

[14] Bible, New Living Translation Psalm 55:22
[15] Bible, New International Version 1 John 4:1

certain matters renders people vulnerable to manipulation, exploitation and control.

In the same ways people are admonished to test the spirits because many false prophets are out in the world, many Christians were and still are either fearful or neglecting to test the information given to them by external authorities about COVID-19, the "vaccines' and now the Central Bank Digital Currency being introduced into their life.

This is despite them having received a spirit that is to set them free from fear or enslavement by evil forces. Yet, with the evil forces ensnaring them in plain sight, they still cannot see how they're instrumental in their own enslavement of a hell on earth they helped to build and effectively had become the guardians of.

Can we make a difference?

Any plan aimed at controlling people requires people to be controlled and other people to do the controlling.

In so far as I identify in this book, those seeking to exercise the controlling are the people who own and control the production of money. You, the ordinary man or woman on the street, who are the large majority, do not own and neither do you control the production of money. If you did, you would have no shortage of it.

The people to be controlled are the rest of us.

The plan is useless without us. In other words, the central bankers need you and me to be their subjects. The plan is not to be exerted upon them. It is to be exerted on you and me. Without us, the plan and its execution would be dead in the water.

Given that we can think and decide for ourselves, it simply requires us to critically evaluate and discuss the current state of affairs in our local communities, our countries and the world as a whole.

In order to address meaningfully these issues which are outside of us, we need to first resolve issues already affecting us on the inside — meaning our individual selves. How do we behave? What currently "comes out of us" and why?

A deep dive into these matters is crucial if we want to understand how and why we behave in the manner that we currently do. It will help us understand how our current environment thrives by what we do and don't —what comes out of us and what does not come out of us.

We need to gain an understanding of the childhood traumas we are laced with on the inside. These traumas, the result of external impact upon us, very much dictate what comes out of us. The sooner we gain insight, we will be better placed to understand one another in our current behavioural form — the response we give others and what we receive from others.

People whose objective it is to manipulate and control us exploit the fact that we are vulnerable because of our traumas. Our unresolved pain sets us up to be risk-averse in relation to one another. Many of our relationships are characterised by being each other's adversaries. The courage to come and work together suffers because our pain of the past conditioned us not to trust each other for fear of repeated pain. We are also easily drawn to situations that appear to provide the emotional fulfilment we've been deprived of. This is how easily we can be drawn in and exploited by people who prey on our emotional vulnerabilities.

Christians say God, the Almighty, is Love. They believe God sent Jesus to save anyone who believes in Jesus. Jesus said to love God above all and your neighbour as yourself. [16] Needless to say, is that Jesus also translates as Love. Therefore, belief in Jesus implies belief in Love. As God is Almighty, then so must love be also. Therefore, whoever believes in Jesus also believes in the power of love.

If you believe in the power of love, applying it would make sense. Also, 1 John 4:20 (Bible, New International Version) states: "Whoever claims to love God yet hates a brother or sister is a liar. For whoever does not love their brother and sister, whom they have seen, cannot love God, whom they have not seen." Therefore, in the face of adversity, love is that potent power to dissolve whatever causes distress.

Love, as stated in 1 Corinthians, is described to have the following characteristics in its discharge:

"Love is patient, love is kind. It does not envy, it does not boast, it is not proud. It does not dishonour others, it is not self-seeking, it is not easily angered, and it keeps no record of wrongs. Love does not delight in evil but rejoices with the truth. It always protects, always trusts, always hopes, always perseveres."[17]

---

[16] Bible, New International Version Matthew 22:37-39
[17] Bible, New International Version, 1 Corinthians 13:4-7

For the Christian believer in God, it is clear what their belief entails for them to do. If Christian believers had never heard of these statements or were never taught about them, it's fair to say that they don't know how to go about applying what they believe or follow. But if they had, it begs the question why they don't do it.

A further question to ask is whether Christians really have faith in these statements and teachings they receive(d).

If they do have faith and do not doubt these statements, it is worth pointing out how powerful Christian faith can be as in Matthew, "Jesus replied, "Truly I tell you, if you have faith and do not doubt, not only can you do what was done to the fig tree, but also you can say to this mountain, 'Go, throw yourself into the sea,' and it will be done."[18]

In the Christian's defence, it may be that the mountain referred to is metaphorical. That metaphorical reference implies matters adversely affecting the person or people's lives and causing them distress and disharmonious living. The problems in their lives. So, by faith, these issues should be resolved.

What is faith? Hewbrews states, "...faith is confidence in what we hope for and assurance about what we do not see."[19] To have confidence implies to trust and have firm belief as opposed to having doubt about something.

---

[18] Bible, New International Version Matthew 21:21
[19] Hewbrews 11:1

At James, it states "What good is it, my brothers and sisters, if someone claims to have faith but has no deeds? Can such faith save them?"[20]

Given these statements, it's fair to ask any Christian the following:

Do you have faith in Jesus Christ? If yes,

Do you carry in you the Spirit of Christ? If yes,

Do you believe in the power of love, which is in the spirit of Christ? if yes,

Do you have faith that the spirit of Christ in you can move the metaphorical mountains causing suffering? If yes,

Do you believe that the discerning power of the spirit allows you to identify evil when it presents itself? If yes,

Do you agree that you cannot serve both God and Mammon? (Bearing in mind that you cannot serve both God and Money as per Matthew, which states, "No one can serve two masters, since either he will hate one and love the other, or he will be devoted to one and despise the other. You cannot serve both God and money."[21] If yes,

Do you believe that money is a creation of Mammon and not of God?— why would God create money if a distinction is drawn between the two and God being the better option?

Given what you now know about how money impacts people's lives, do you believe that Central Bank Digital

---

[20] Bible, New International Version James 2:14
[21] Christian Standard Bible Matthew 6:24

Currency (CBDC) is that very instrument that seeks to enslave God's people? If yes,

What and how are you doing to apply the power of your Faith and of Love to alleviate suffering amongst your neighbours and to stop such or any other evil from being reintroduced and accepted into the day-to-day activities of our society?

Another effect of money:

Money is a notable instrument that interferes with our human spirit to love and be kind to one another. The fact is that without money, we can still be growing, harvesting and sharing food crops with others around us and even exporting to countries where people may lack such crops.

The development of technology and transport would still operate perfectly well as the resources themselves do not require money to function in the way that it does. Oil won't stop working just because people aren't using money to access, refine or distribute it. The same goes for electricity. It won't stop working just because people aren't paying for it or nobody makes a monetary profit from it. The same applies to every other resource being traded for money.

Without money, there'd also be no need for war or the infringement of the fulfilment of anyone's existential needs. The argument that some would simply resign to being lazy on not wanting to do anything while others do all the work is another expression of distrust — which is not borne out of love. We can be better motivated by making it a joy to do and participate in that which makes life enjoyable for us all and simply discontinue activities which do not amount to such ends.

We can travel the world and exchange people to come and go to learn about methods of production of certain items we all can benefit from. This is fulfilling to the human mind, for we are purpose-driven and sharing knowledge which keeps us all safe and fulfilling needs everywhere. The more we learn, the better for future generations about how to survive and conduct an enjoyable existence in harmony with our fellowmen as opposed to competition, which leads to the disadvantageous outcomes we needlessly battle with political euphemisms as a response. It's obvious that we're locked in a tug of war wherever money serves to regulate.

If we engaged kindness as currency for human interactions, our mental and overall health would improve overnight.

That's the power of love. There'd be peace because we serve each other's best interests. Loving our neighbours as we love ourselves — the ends of which are benign and constructive. Not destructive.

Chapter 8

Social Conscience

Contemporary society operates almost like a metaphorical human mind. It has a conscious and unconscious element.

The unconscious is the vast sum of operations of the mind that take place below the level of conscious awareness. The conscious mind contains all the thoughts, feelings, cognitions, and memories we acknowledge, while the unconscious consists of deeper mental processes not readily available to the conscious mind.[22]

To be conscious is to be aware of one's surroundings and being responsive to them. The unconscious part of our mind is what the conscious does not readily access but nonetheless affects our emotions and behaviours.

To be unconscious also means that one is not able to respond to people and your surroundings. One exists and does things, but without realising.

Likewise, an unconscious societal part also exists. Although it may not apply conscious or critical thinking, it nonetheless affects activities in the social environment.

The unconscious element of society is what conscious society suppresses to advance what it considers to be a better society

---

[22] https//www.psychologytoday.com

—that part of society which it does not like about itself and thus suppresses, silences and tries to control for the sake of its selective consciousness. But because it is a part that won't go away, it sometimes pays attention by listening to some of its demands. These demands are only addressed to the extent that the dominant preferred ways are not overthrown.

Here, we can think of campaigns prior to elections. Some of society's actions are consciously targeted at starving some of the "unwanted" or "unpopular" to prevent interference with its current ways.

In some autocratic societies, maiming and killing of the non-conforming is the norm. In democratic capitalistic societies, we see threats and propaganda and the extreme carried out by organised militia. So, it blocks this unwanted, unpopular part of society out of view to project a preferred state of affairs. A dysfunctional form of denial is the prevailing response to suffering within itself.

Parts of society are so unaware that when presented with a question for the solution of some of the emerging problems emanating from the unwanted parts, it gives unsuitable shortsighted replies as a solution. Here, one can look at the alleged historical response of Mary Antoinette (French Queen) when she was told that the people did not have any bread to eat. She allegedly said, "Give them cake."

Though the governments of the day are more aware of the problems in the unpopular section of society, they still introduce solutions which does nothing to address the fundamental problem. For instance, unhealthy food is cheaper and more readily available than healthy ones. When informed about the problems these foods cause, they see increasing the tax on these foods as the solution.

While shortsightedness is the prevailing approach, complete blindness holds true for others.

The idea of making healthy food available and accessible to all simply eludes consensus. Central to governing bodies' conscious thinking is that of financial impact. Money has become a pivotal factor in decision-making. It is no wonder why the individual's orientation and strive is no different. When a dispute erupts over an appeal to help the destitute, money takes centre stage.

The ongoing dispute is shaped by conflict between modern-day society and its unresolved past. The repeated inhospitable outcomes are the manifestations thereof. Many arguments in objection to taking responsibility for this ongoing social problem are rooted in selfishness disguised in plausible deniability.

These are the unwilling patrons who have passionately fallen in love with the notion that everybody will eventually find their way to the top with hard work. Blatantly overlooked is the fact that the propagated ladder to the top is a construction site operated with the tormented living of those forced to accept less or nothing at all. This belief normalises harm to others and perversely rationalises it as progress or "for the good of society." With closer inspection, it becomes very obvious that this "progress" is destructive.

The destructive nature of this belief and practice remains the denial of those who live in the thick cloud of ignorance or pretentious consciousness, obscuring the light from what really matters.

The Bible[23] story of Jesus feeding five thousand people with five loaves of bread and two fish inspires an attitude of care and sharing with one's neighbour. The story demonstrates an authority of a different orientation to the internal and external authorities driving contemporary society.

Much of the public remains unconscious of its participation in and advocating of two opposing sets of norms— that of charitable Christian altruism and bourgeois indifference and selfishness.

When brought to the attention of the social conscience, the initial response is no different from how we treat "the unconscious part" of our being — denial and suppression. This cycle of behaviour is perpetuated by responses of individuals and groups uncourageous and afraid to challenge the status quo.

Our divided selves

Belonging is a basic human need. If this need is not fulfilled, people become isolated and risk an imbalance in their mental and overall health.

In an age of social media, the craving for connectedness, approval and acceptance is blatantly obvious. For many, the use of social media itself is an expression of a craving for belonging to a crowd, without which the individual

---

[23] John 6:1-13

experiences exclusion. It has become the modern standard for defining who you are. Without a social media profile, you're almost considered to not exist. People reach out far more and easier to people via the medium of a social media device as opposed to direct personal contact for natural interpersonal.

Disconnectedness seems easily cured by posting a picture of oneself, often edited for aesthetic appeal, to attract interaction, acceptance and belonging. Low self esteem also seems to undergo instant cure as people "like" the picture posted. The person having posted the picture of themselves bathing in the online responses as confirmation that they're liked and approved of.

With deeper inspection, one discovers that the "likes" interpreted as approval are not necessarily a true reflection of how people feel or associate with the person in the picture. The picture represents a moment captured in the life of the person in the picture. The expression reflected in the picture may or may not be true. Photo sessions tend to give an impression of how the person feels or a statement that provokes feelings in the viewer. The effect on the viewer may or may not be intended for by the person who posted the picture. It is also true in many cases that whatever the picture may convey is not a true reflection of the life or personality of the person in the picture.

Commercial oriented society has refined the art of making something appealing, and the same tactics are applied in human relations. People effectively now put themselves up for sale in the popularity market for approval and acceptance, hoping to achieve many "likes" perceived as currency for validating themselves in society.

The popularity market that social media, in many ways, has become now determines people's "value" in society. To be unpopular is painful and negates being wanted, belonging or fitting in.

Engagement in the economy, job interviews, and even dating are now affected by your social media personality status as opposed to your true self. We effectively operate the disapproval of our authentic self for the advancement of a manufactured version of ourselves. We somehow define better by the admiration value of personality-altering accessories hyped up by commercial propaganda as essential for social validation.

The job

The activities

The food

The gadgets

The cars

The membership/association

The places to be at

The physical appearance, clothing and makeup

The tattoo

The house

The style/fashion

The attitude, mood and feelings

Etcetera, Etcetera...

In other words, these now determine your personal social status.

A palpable air of competition lurks as people hustle for attention in their bid for popularity and acceptance. The end of which is to gain an advantage over others to maximise their own personal consumption — whether it is for tangible items or feeding an emotional hunger created by their past, all of which is patronisingly entertained by a growing sense of avariciousness in society.

Chapter 9

Relationships

The basis of how people relate and respond to one another is often their individual trauma inflicted upon them in the course of their lives —usually in childhood.

It is due to either something that happened that shouldn't have or something that ought to have happened but didn't.[24]

The impact of these events condition the individual's mind and thus their subsequent response to any situation that triggers their trauma. These behaviours are carried through into adulthood. If people are not aware of their own trauma, they will not understand the root of their behaviours and responses to other people. Things people do or don't do, say or don't say, are likely to evoke an emotional reaction which sets people off.

Adverse childhood events are the markers that set us up for sensitivities in later life. These events vary for different people. Some people may experience a few in the course of their childhood, while others experience far more.

Adverse Childhood Experiences (ACEs) are "highly stressful, and potentially traumatic, events or situations that occur during childhood and/or adolescence. They can be a

---

[24] Dr Gabor Maté

single event or prolonged threats to, and breaches of, the young person's safety, security, trust or bodily integrity."[25]

Examples of ACEs are:

- Physical Abuse

- Sexual Abuse

- Emotional Abuse

- Living with someone who abused drugs

- Living with someone who abused alcohol

- Exposure to domestic violence

- Living with someone who has gone to prison

- Living with someone with serious mental illness

- Losing a parent through divorce, death or abandonment

Experiencing ACEs can have an impact on our future physical and mental health, and often, ACEs can be barriers to healthy attachment relationships forming for children. Some of the effects of ACEs on our physical and mental health are:

- An increase in the risk of certain health problems in adulthood, such as cancer and heart disease, as well as

---

[25] Young Minds, 2018

increasing the risk of mental health difficulties, violence and becoming a victim of violence.

• An increase in the risk of mental health problems, such as anxiety, depression, and post-traumatic stress. According to the National Health Service in the UK, 1 in 3 diagnosed mental health conditions in adulthood directly relate to ACEs.

• The longer an individual experiences an ACE and the more ACEs someone experiences, the bigger the impact it will have on their development and their health.

Some of the other things exposure to ACEs can impact are:

• The ability to recognise and manage different emotions.

• The capacity to make and keep healthy friendships and other relationships.

• The ability to manage behaviour in school settings.

Difficulties coping with emotions safely without causing harm to self or others.

People who lack insight into the impact that adverse experiences have on an individual would struggle to forge and maintain a therapeutic relationship with someone suffering from trauma. In many cases, both parties are unaware and have no insight, and their relationship becomes the unintended perfect recipe for endless conflict and an unpleasant life experience.

Children born out of these relationships and being raised by such already afflicted parents will, in due course, become affected to become the unsuspecting torchbearers of generational trauma. A toxic emotional environment that almost certainly guarantees children the adverse experiences to which societal groups such as churches so desperately pray they don't fall victim.

Add to that the pressure and lack of money for the fulfilment of their basic human needs, and you have the perfect storm which makes for the volatile society we see.

A praying church and existing government-funded institutions whose complicit participation in the commercial-oriented societal order render them ineffective saviours for the complex problems.

Married couples divorce.

Families are torn apart.

Children are taken into foster care or end up in jail.

People succumb to substance abuse in an effort to cope.

People cause themselves and or others harm in physical, emotional, sexual or financial abuse.

Adverse Childhood Experiences can be highly limiting to a person's potential. It has the ability to trap you in a state of neurosis, and you end up repeating the same behaviours only under different circumstances. The conditioning that ACEs affords the individual makes them vulnerable to any external stimuli that trigger their sensitivity and automates the process that leads them down a path of behaviours that journeys them to the same point at which they hope to not repeat the same behaviours.

Unless the individual takes serious pause and thinks critically about their own conditioning with the view to really understand their own condition and vulnerability and to take constructive actions for better internal adjustment and coping, they will repeat an experience of life and the world around them in context of the pain they desperately try to escape but never do. In other words, you'd repeatedly be chasing after different opportunities, all of which amount to short-lived moments of excitement and happiness on the surface that fail to penetrate to the core where it's really needed.

Politicians exploit these desperate circumstances by making promises they cannot fulfil. Politicians themselves are often individuals afflicted with much trauma in their own lives. Where they suffered deprivation themselves, they're either motivated to help others or help themselves escape the harsh conditions they were plunged into by the political system they lived under enforced.

South Africa is a typical example of a people who, due to colonisation, suffered a torrent of adverse events inflicted upon them by the social and economic order of Apartheid. It affected people mentally in that some adopted or were conditioned to adopt a superiority complex, whilst others developed an inferiority complex.

These opposites invariably set people up in an adversarial stance towards one another. It was typically based on the colour of people's skin, where persons with lighter skin colour, the legal system classified as white, were given economic privileges that people who were classified as black or coloured were not afforded by the government of the day.

The social order supported by the economic order (and vice versa) conditioned many people of white classification to consider people with other skin colour of lesser importance. While this may not hold true for all people who are classified as white, the impact upon the psyche of those who are classified as non-white was profound, and the adverse effects remain to this day.

The impact was not just limited to that of people's psyche but also affected their socio-economic circumstances. People who were classified as coloured and black typically occupied lower-ranking roles in teaching, police, correctional service, social work, nursing, cleaning, labourers etc. The income provided by the roles created a state of want, which kept them loyal to doing exactly that for fear of losing what they had. Amongst the coloured community one easily finds several generations of teachers or police in the same family.

Typically, you'd find a married couple consisting of a police officer and a nurse or a police officer and a teacher or two teachers.

The higher ranking and higher paying jobs were the reserves of people of white classification. Very few people who are classified as black and coloured could pursue higher ranking and higher paying jobs. When they did, and when they achieved such positions, they tended to adopt the same superiority complex which they go on to discharge against other people.

Also typical, is the gleeful celebration when people of black or coloured classification achieve an award, join a prestigious school or achieve a qualification such as a doctor, lawyer or chief executive role formally reserved for people of white classification. These are often the expressions of wanting or having to prove themselves better than what others thought or had been made to think of themselves.

One such example is a person publicly sworn in as the mayor of my hometown, Beaufort West. He cried and went to thank his mother for the title and position he was appointed into. His mother was seemingly overwhelmed by what she clearly had no hand in manoeuvring but for the power play of local politics. He occupied the role for only a few months before being replaced by another person who also didn't occupy the same position for too long before being manoeuvred out. This cycle repeated itself with five people for the same role.

The African National Congress (ANC), which took government office in 1994, is a clear display of how corrupted human relations had become. They stood on a pledge to govern for the well-being and benefit of all South African citizens. South Africa was referred to as the "Rainbow Nation," a term coined by Desmond Tutu (Anglican Archbishop). Over the course of three decades, the ANC-Government has presided over a plethora of corrupt activities that saw the mismanagement of public funds for the benefit of a few people (see The State Capture Report). Explicit was the rise in people who were formally classified as white joining the ranks of desperately poor people.

It tells the story of strained human relations that have people working against each other as opposed to for one another.

The contempt between people of white, black and coloured classification is rarely extinguished even as they occupy the same job ranks because of the implicit bias imprinted by their personal and joint past.

As the vicious cycle takes its toll, the pressure exerted by money means for one's living, only makes matters worse. Where there's a need to rehabilitate, it suffers under the strain of affordability. Poor public service manufactured by corporate lobbying that seeks to maximise their profits through privatisation of essential services are underlying factors that keep society trapped in a matrix of all forms of abuse.

In other words — Hell on earth.

Chapter 10

Racism

The Oxford Dictionary defines racism as prejudice, discrimination, or antagonism by an individual, community, or institution against a person or people on the basis of their membership of a particular racial or ethnic group, typically one that is a minority or marginalised.

Given the history of human relations between people of white ethnicity and those of black ethnicity, the above definition bears relevance. With reference to the history of South African politics, it is the case that people of white ethnicity designed and discharged social affairs prejudicially against people who were not classified as being of white ethnicity. The history is vast and has no shortage of horror stories that resulted in various forms of abuse against people.

In light of the above definition and reference, let's examine whether the definition as it stands and that of the factual reference to South African history holds true for contemporary society and whether the original definition's emphasis —that of prejudice against people on the basis of racial or ethnic group was a true and holistic accurate capturing for the term racism to be understood.

The local management of South African politics changed hands in 1994 when, as a result of a general election, the African National Congress (ANC) occupied the position of government. At the time of publishing of this book, the ANC had been in government office for well over three decades. The general social perception was that the ANC government was to end racism and establish a societal environment where prejudice against any person, particularly purely based on racial and ethnic group, was abolished. The record shows the abolishing of legislation which enshrined prejudice against people on the basis of racial or ethnic group.

However, the record of conduct by the ANC government in many of its ministers for the discharge of politics to end racism is not only disputed by anecdotal evidence but also a fact, as discovered by the state capture inquiry and current events shaping the political landscape. The state capture inquiry revealed corruption − that of the fraudulent acquisition and management of public assets and funds, and such assets and funds being channelled for the disproportionate benefit of groups and persons who predominantly were not of white ethnicity. The state capture report is voluminous. Readers are encouraged to read the details for records of activities that did not serve the public's best interest or for the advancing of public confidence that racism is being ended.

In public circles, the term "reverse racism" had become a common theme for objectively judging the effect of the political adjustments since the ANC government came into office. It is the case that many people of white ethnicity now face the harsh reciprocation of their interests not being prioritised. As to whether that is purely because of their race or ethnic group is open for debate. There is anecdotal evidence of stories not necessarily entertained by national news and then there is evidence by way of legislative changes.

The Employment Equity Act, 55 of 1998 provides for the redress of the disparity in employment as a result of the Apartheid Era Laws, which saw people of black ethnicity excluded from certain and or higher positions of employment. This law requires that employers give equal opportunity and ensure the employment of people from designated groups. Designated groups are defined in section 1 of the Act as "black people, women and people with disabilities." Worth noting is that although the government that presided over Apartheid laws (Population Act, 30 of 1950) specified at least three distinct races —"white," "black," and "coloured"— the ANC government went on to define "black people" as a generic term which means Africans, Coloureds and Indians. (section 1 of the Employment Equity Act).

Affirmative action saw the radical implementation of measures that catapulted people formerly classified as "black" into positions of employment proportionately more than those who were formerly classified as "coloured" and, in many cases, to the total exclusion of people who formally identified as "white." A statistical analysis done by Rhodes University[26] breaks down the radical shift in employment and unemployment in South Africa from 1994-2024 based on

---

[26] https://www.ru.ac.za/facultyofcommerce/ latestnews/jobdisparitiesaccordingtoracearealarming.html

data published by the South African Department for Statistics.[27]

Anecdotal evidence of people who lost their jobs and could not get a job under the measure of affirmative action speaks of direct discrimination against them on the grounds of their race. The fact that legislative changes were specific in addressing the disparities, that disparity was clear —race and ethnic group. Affirmative action is the semantic branding for reversed race discrimination with people of white ethnicity being the target for disadvantage.

What really were the driving factors for race discrimination in the previous era of government? Was it really a desire to live separate from people of black ethnicity? If it was, it begs the question as to why the British and the Dutch went to South Africa and other countries where the people were not predominantly of white ethnicity when they already had countries from where they originated. They even uprooted people in Africa and took them by force to Europe, where they made them work as slaves. The answer is unambiguously clear —the acquisition and control of land rich in mineral resources and thereby gain economic advantage. The formulation of laws that separated people on the grounds of their ethnicity within the same country was an evil genius plan that ensured ring-fenced management, control and enjoyment of material wealth at the expense of those disadvantaged by the arrangement.

---

[27] https://www.statssa.gov.za/?p=17266

Although the moral outcry against the despicable disparities created by racism demanded the restoration of human rights and dignity for people not classified as "white," the implemented measures such as affirmative action and "black economic empowerment" remain an ineffective answer for the practical restoration of human rights and dignity for all South Africans and other people across the world. The declaration that all are equal in terms of the law means nothing when human dignity suffers decimation on a daily basis.

The classic definition of "racism" is somewhat misleading for what racism really is. It excludes a vital element without which its practice historically and in contemporary society has no prominence. It only draws attention to prejudice with emphasis on race and ethnic groups. It implies that racism has no other premise or part. It implies that racism can only exist if it is levelled against someone who is not of the same race or ethnic group as the one discharging it.

Think of the word "race" as a competition between at least two parties for a prize and "racism" as the environment it thrives in. This emphasis on context draws us closer to the root and origins as opposed to the same spelling with context fixation on ethnic groups.

A flower without nurturing from its roots wouldn't bloom. Racism has roots, too. Those roots are imperialism and economic antagonism. The undeniable "flower" of racism is the economic deprivation of individuals or groups of people.

Racism, at its root, is actually defined as a competitive economic struggle between groups of people for power and wealth. It remains alive to this day. Neither the ANC-government nor any other country has ended racism. It can be seen that governments effectively keep racism alive, and it is no longer solely premised on the basis of your race or ethnic group. The flower of racism in South Africa decimates the dignity of people across all racial lines. When people cannot access basic necessities for their dignified living due to economic deprivation, racism is effectively levelled at them.

Employment is semantics for slavery. You only give written consent to be exploited by the slave master now termed your "employer."

It is the effect and outcomes that really give definition to a term or word.

The widely accepted definition of racism is a convenient construct which misdirects attention from the root whilst the evidence of racism, a despicable practice antagonising human dignity, is in plain sight.

Chapter 11

Hell

There are various definitions and descriptions of what the hell is.

According to the Dictionary of Oxford Languages, hell is a place regarded in various religions as a spiritual realm of evil and suffering, often traditionally depicted as a place of perpetual fire beneath the earth where the wicked are punished after death.

In the Bible, hell has many descriptions and meaning across many books and verses. Matthew defines it as a place of "...outer darkness, where there will be weeping and gnashing of teeth."[28]

Not a pleasant place or destination for one's residency or journey through or afterlife. Hell is often also used to describe people's current life experiences and is not strictly an experience reserved for the afterlife of those who didn't obey God the Almighty. If one were to take the bible's description of what the hell is, that is an experience many people already can testify of. Look at the physical and emotional living conditions that many people are in. Amongst them, many attend church and profess their belief in God. Some of their spiritual "brothers and sisters" live in

---

[28] Matthew 25:301

vastly comfortable physical surroundings and are not afflicted by conditions that can be described as hell for those lacking material affluence.

Of course, there is emotional well-being, which is also attributed to one's experience of life. It could be "heaven," or it could be "hell." There can be no doubt that many people experience life in this sphere to be more hell than heaven. Considering the emotional trauma they carry from their childhood — issues that remain unaddressed and, in many cases, never spoken about. These are the harms done to people regardless of whether they grew up in material affluence or abject socio-economic poverty. Whatever happened continues to haunt many to this day.

The unfortunate truth is that what happens never leaves the mind. The impact of whatever happened to someone manifests in their behaviours affecting their relationships with partners, children, family and other people in general.

Take, for example, someone who had been sexually abused during their childhood. That sexual abuse could even include having been raped or subjected to attempted rape. That may be one of their earliest experience of hell. Given a safe space without being judged, many would talk about their encounters with sexual abuse at the hands of people they reasonably believed they could trust. These incidents vary in particular, but what they all have in common is the lasting impact on the abused. Such people find themselves burdened with deep-seated emotional issues ranging from distrust of others and seeking emotional security often exhibited in sexual promiscuity. How people present their behaviours as a consequence isn't confined to only that of sexual promiscuity but can exhibit many other coping mechanisms, such as abuse of substances such as alcohol and or drugs. A deep one-to-one conversation with such affected persons would bring forth the horror stories and reveal the emotional hell they face on a daily basis.

Society has varied responses to the plight of people affected by abuse in their childhood. Many don't want to hear it because it often triggers unpleasant memories about their own similar experience, which they suppress as a coping mechanism. Such suppression is often managed or concealed by way of staunch religious practice orientation in the belief that it would either dissolve or absolve them from the pain—that God will heal them and help them forgive the perpetrator —a place of refuge, but often in the same breath hope that God would deal with the perpetrator as reckoning for what the perpetrator did.

Other attitudes in society are to shame the person claiming to have been abused and even accuse them of having wanted it to happen or asserting that it was God's punishment for something they did wrong. The rationale people give varies greatly. These are but a few examples of the unhelpful responses to other people's suffering found in society. Our legal justice system is more focused on punishing perpetrators as opposed to looking into why things happened — confronting the conditions that lead to such outcomes.

Purgatory is another place of reservation according to the catholic church doctrine. It implies that you'd have another chance to make amends and have your sins forgiven before going to heaven. The catholic church and other projects as holding the keys that could unlock the gates of heaven if only you subjected yourself to their instruction.

Such church and similar beliefs regarding heaven display an obvious disregard for the factors and role it plays in enabling the very conditions people are to be saved from. It's quite clear that the catholic church and others possess vast amounts of material wealth which could feed the hungry and house the homeless as a very small gesture. Instead, they horde and pay homage to other materially wealthy people who's economic activities are instrumental in creating the physical and emotional turmoil which renders people to seek solace where they're left begging for pardon to achieve presumed lasting peace.

Is hell really a place of fire and brimstone where one burns forever? Think about it. What type of body burns but is never destroyed by the fire? If you're never going to be consumed by the fire, what's the point of being cast into it? Isn't this another form of emotional abuse levelled at people desperate for relief from the actual hell manufactured by money management of society, of which the church is a silent partner but presents itself as an instrument of saving? Is the threat of hell a means of conditioning people into obeying the church whose obvious complacency actually deserves dissolution?

As christian churches aspire for people to do introspection and make internal adjustments, I make the case that it would be socially useful for them to set that example. Such an example could start by ceasing the collection of money from people, instead encouraging followers to help their neighbours directly and join efforts for the complete removal of the concept and order of any form of money in society — because money is partly the fuel that keeps the "hell fire" burning.[29]

[29] Bible, New International Version

Chapter 12

Knowledge And Power

There is the belief that knowledge is power. But is it true?

Knowledge is the fact or condition of knowing something with familiarity gained through experience or association.[30]

Power is the ability to act or produce an effect.[31]

I have looked into this statement and found that many people know about many things yet are in a state of paralysis to effect the changes they desire in their lives. They are captured by circumstances that render them just enough oxygen to think and speak of what they know or say to believe. Despite their knowledge, their internal and external environment reflects little to no effect on what they claim to believe in.

Believing in something doesn't make it a fact. A belief and a fact are two different postulations. Belief denotes something that is accepted, considered to be true or held as an opinion. Fact denotes what is proven to be true.

Having observed people who have either the same, different or even less knowledge than others but apply what they know

---

[30] Merriam-Webster Dictionary
[31] Ibid

because of their practical belief therein, they shape their internal and external environment, which amounts to the outcomes they experience.

So, what we actually do is really what makes the difference. What we do also reflects what we really believe in —that which is dominant or strong in us. What otherwise holds true for many are wishes, pretentiousness or a preferred state of mind as opposed to dealing with reality.

Therefore, knowledge isn't power. It is the application of knowledge that is the power because it is what produces the outcomes we see. Even the misapplication of that knowledge produces an outcome. Merely having knowledge is like having a gun and bullets but never loading the bullets into the gun or firing it. All too familiar is the growing number of university graduates who remain unemployed due to varied factors of which economic forces play a central role.

Many Christians say that there is power in the blood of Jesus and claim to have been "washed by the blood of Jesus." Metaphorical, of course. Yet, when you put it to them to love their neighbour, the majority fail to make the obvious practical application. They struggle within themselves to make the internal adjustment first. Their concern or complaint is more that of the outside world. They want things to change outside of themselves first before they can adjust. If that were to be the condition for people to change, they'd merely be reacting and not responding. Reference to Matthew, "And why do you look at the speck in your brother's eye, but do not consider the plank in your own eye?"[32] is often used only as a metaphor for discouraging judgement of others. However, this metaphor can also be a powerful reference for Christians to portray the lack of practical activity on their own part to effect a societal environment of brotherly love as opposed to complacency to the transactional exchanges, which strains human relations and destroys human life.

To respond is a form of taking responsibility. In other words, you'd have to have the ability to respond – therefor, response-able or response-ability.

An ability to respond to your circumstances requires that you have insight and understanding of what you're faced with or dealing with. Without that necessary insight and understanding, you'd be open to misdirection. Having the relevant knowledge with insight and understanding positions one better to know what needs to be done and how to avoid the current state of affairs pitfalls that befall you. You can thus make decisions with well-thought reasons. It means that you exercise critical thinking and not just leave it to mysticism or fate, as some people resign themselves to.

The leadership in many churches is often where the root obstacles are. They operate the Church fundamentally as a means for enriching themselves. They exploit people's emotional deprivations by guilt-tripping them about the need for internal adjustment and obedience to Jesus and the Church, which they, the Church Leaders, ultimately represent. Telling people to give money to the church is

---

[32] Matthew 7:3

money that goes into their pockets to secure their living and lifestyle — effectively trading gospel for money.

If we really want to make a positive difference in our personal lives and that of our neighbours, then we need to apply the constructive knowledge of love. The power of love would be seen for the effect it has. It is the case that many church leaders are more in love with the power of authority. They exploit this position as a direct result of irrational fear they generate through the perversion of the gospel—often being selective in application and directing it to apply to congregants except themselves.

If the church was to make any useful, practical and effective impact for necessary societal change, church leaders would have to operate the church for the sole benefit of the public's emotional and spiritual fulfilment. All and any material wealth should be directed toward the fulfilment of the public's physiological needs, such as shelter, food and water. The immediate practical application would be to use all the money or goods collected at church for distribution amongst the evidently needy in our communities. For the avoidance of issues, church goers should be encouraged to simply bring food, clothing and other items needed to alleviate the physiological deprivations suffered by people in the community — meaning alleviate poverty.

Church, should be an organisation of people who teach and convey information about love and organising groups of people to bring information and items of need to others lacking necessities for living. Everyone needs Love. Everyone needs shelter, food, water, clothing and other necessities for daily living. People attending church can offer their food, materials, skills and talents for free—all of which goes to alleviate the "poverty" in their communities. Concerns about the people simply sitting and waiting to be served are the mindset of the commercially oriented who believe that people only deserve something if they've done something for it. This mindset is what occupies the thinking of many Christians, forgetting that based on their own principles of faith, Jesus gave up his life without conditions to those who are the benefactors. The commercial mindset, doing something for someone else only if you get something in return, poisons people's ability to effect love in themselves and others or establish loving relations with others.

Some people possess the ability to teach, build or grow food, amongst other talents. People with a talent, for example, singing or performing, can bring this to the community for enjoyment and not ask for monetary reward but bathe in the difference they make and reciprocate the joy of their loving act. The same goes for many other skills.

A church building should be owned by the community. Not privately. This privately owned church mentality gives rise to the commercial orientation and activities that distort what the churches ought to be operating with and for —the gospel of love to sustain a caring community.

The local Municipalities already have the necessary assets to facilitate their communities' needs, culture and religious beliefs. These buildings can be used for such purposes and also adapted to suit the religious beliefs operating in the community. The South African Constitution provides under s.15(2) of Chapter 2 for people's right to religious freedom and that religious observances can be conducted at state-aided institutions.

Given a municipality's current local governing structure, existing laws can be utilised to bring such a culture to life. The local governing structure has provisions for the public to participate in governing the affairs of their local Municipalities. The Municipal Systems Act, 32 of 2000, in section 2(b)(ii), defines a municipality as inclusively consisting of the community.

The South African Municipal Systems Act, Act 32 of 2000, was written with a clear intention to uplift people from the socio-economic injustice of the apartheid era with emphasis on the poor and disadvantaged in the community.

It provides for the core principles, mechanisms and processes that are necessary to

— enable municipalities to move progressively towards the social and economic upliftment of local communities and ensure universal access to essential services that are affordable to all;

— to define the legal nature of a municipality as including the local community within the municipal area, working in partnership with the municipality's political and administrative structures;

— to provide for the manner in which municipal powers and functions are exercised and performed;

— to provide for community participation;

— to establish a simple and enabling framework for the core processes of planning, performance management, resource mobilisation and organisational change, which underpin the notion of developmental local government;

— to provide a framework for local public administration and human resource development;

— to empower the poor and ensure that municipalities put in place service tariffs and credit control policies that take their needs into account by providing a framework for the provision of services, service delivery agreements and municipal service districts;

— to provide for credit control and debt collection;

— to establish a framework for support, monitoring and standard-setting by other spheres of government in order to progressively build local government into an efficient, frontline development agency capable of integrating the activities of all spheres of government for the overall social and economic upliftment of communities in harmony with their local natural environment;

A poignant provision for the practical realisation of changes in the community is section 16(1)(c) of the Municipal Systems Act, which provides that the Municipality must use its resources and annually allocate funds in its budget as may be appropriate for the purposes of implementing subsections (a) and (b).

Subsection (a) requires that the municipality encourage and create conditions for the local community to participate in the affairs of the municipality. It allows the community to participate in:

• 	(i) the preparation, implementation and review of its integrated development plan in terms of Chapter 5.

Chapter 5 (section 21(b) of the Municipal Systems Act, Act 32 of 2000) requires the municipality to give effect to its developmental duties required by section 153 of the South African Constitution. Section 153 states that a municipality must structure and manage its administration, budgeting and planning processes to prioritise the community's basic needs and promote the community's social and economic development.

Section 16(1) is a crucial part of the local government legislation, enabling the community to make decisions about critical matters affecting them. It is the point at which the community's needs and priorities can jointly be identified as opposed to being assumed. No plan can be implemented as appropriate and or targeted for community benefit if the community's views and input are not incorporated. In many cases, the community may not have a clue about this provision and are often invited to a meeting in which they do not understand items on the agenda under discussion.

Municipal managers often fail to make information clear and or easy to understand for the local community to enable them to participate. Suppose municipalities carry out their legal duty to encourage and create conditions for the local community to participate. In that case, careful consideration must be had for the cognition of the people in the community. When this is applied, planning and preparation should, in many cases, take a lot longer to ensure the community knows what is agreed upon to happen before implementation.

Where a community finds that their Municipality is engaging processes that do not prioritise or address their needs, this part of the law also gives right to the community to review what the municipality is doing. The law permits the municipality to annually avail funding for purposes that help the community review and address matters impacting upon them.

Food insecurity is an increasing problem, with many people who cannot access employment to secure an income to buy food. Due to low income, others in employment also struggle to adequately fulfil their needs despite the constitutionally protected right to food and other necessities such as safe drinking water.

Suppose the fulfilment of these rights is inseparably tied to a person's commercial viability and employment earnings. In that case, it raises a serious question about the intention of the law behind this right. A must question is: Is the law's intention primarily aimed at preserving commercial activity or human life?

Subsection 16(1)(b) of the Municipal Systems Act requires the municipality to contribute to building the capacity of the local community to enable it to participate in the affairs of the municipality, and councillors and staff must foster community participation. To be blunt, money can and must be used to support community efforts to help the municipality function better, serving the people as a means of prioritising their needs. Nobody has to suffer in any form.

The law also makes it clear that the community's participation must not be interpreted as interfering with the municipal council's right to govern and execute the executive and legislative authority of the municipality. This could be read in two ways, dependent on what one considers a priority. One way is that the municipal council could execute decisions in their sole discretion because they are the executive part of the municipal body. If someone with a strictly commercial and authoritative orientation occupied office in the executive, we are likely to see decisions and delivery of service far from giving priority to the community's input and needs.

Another view is that the community should not be seen as interfering but that their participation is both legal and necessary for the correct discharge of public service that gives priority to the community's basic needs. If people with a loving and caring orientation occupy public office, discharging decisions and services prioritising the public's input and basic needs would be obvious.

It is very obvious that large pockets of the general public do not have the necessary knowledge about the law that governs their rights and responsibilities. It is also the case that many political appointees, whether by way of local, provincial or national elections, also do not have the necessary knowledge about the laws that govern the office they occupy or that which impacts the public they propose to serve. Another sad fact is that some people in the administrative employ of local, provincial and national government service delivery suffer the same lack of knowledge and understanding for the effective discharge of their duties. This very real problem serves to enable the disproportionate and ill-balance of power between governing bodies and the people. More so is the evident "elephant in the room"-exploitation, which sees the development and application of law which in reality prioritises commercial arrangements which renders vast numbers of people powerless consumers of services they have no real control over, whilst being virtue signalled by propaganda that keeps an illusion of freedom and democracy alive.

People's insecurities are effectively manufactured and maintained by a belief that money is necessary and good for regulating human affairs.

Euphemisms by politicians, church and commercial interest orientation only serve to obscure reality, soothe cognitive dissonance and pacify the real power and freedom inherent in a life governed by true love and care for our fellow human beings.

Here's a thought:

Matthew 6:26,

Look at the birds of the air, for they neither sow nor reap nor gather into barns; yet your heavenly Father feeds them. Are you not of more value than they?

Chapter 13

Love, The Solution

Love can be defined in many ways. Many books have been written on the subject, proving that love is broad in definition, has many forms and is diverse in its application. To name a few: Motherly Love, Fatherly Love, Godly Love, Brotherly or Neighbourly Love, Romantic Love, Artistic Love etcetera. It amounts to the active concern for the life and growth of that which one loves. Here, I shall direct the case to that of people — particularly brotherly or neighbourly love.

Important is to be loving. By being loving, I refer to actions and outcomes which amount to the equal and equitable consideration of another person's life and needs, so as to not deprive or cause the deprivation of another person's existential needs.

Far too many of us are needlessly in a state of want. This creates insecurity in not only the people deprived of what they need for their existence, but also in those who already have what they need for their sustenance. Those without are at risk of ill health, and those who have been constantly on their guard, having to protect what they have — hence, insecure. If we produced for the fulfilment of everyone's needs, there'd be no need for insecurity because we'd essentially be operating from a position of care and responsibility for everyone.

Care is a fundamental aspect of love. When we care about ourselves and others we do that which serves our best interest. Caring leads to constructive as opposed to destructive outcomes. We build stronger human bonds which provide for security and nurture our survival and ultimate enjoyment of life. Our outlook for life is brighter because hope for the good would not be unrealistic. We work together to make things happen as we explore and discover the deeper benefits of human interaction emanating from caring for each other.

Responsibility is closely linked with caring for one another. When we accept responsibility for what needs to be done, we need not entertain blame, which makes for difficult human relations. The bible story of Adam and Eve is a classic example of how needless dispute erupts when no one wants to take responsibility for what needs to be done. It's unpleasant to be held accountable for something that went wrong. Unpleasant situations are resolved when we take responsibility for whatever happened to help anyone afflicted by an unpleasant outcome. Responsibility implies being responsive to the needs that arise out of the situation. Unpleasant situations eventually affect us all because of our interdependence. One person's discomfort left unattended or ignored interferes with our human equilibrium for a peaceful or pleasant experience of life. Responding to another's need is good for us all because we restore what could otherwise be a disturbance leading to destructive outcomes. Our responsiveness as a responsibility for others serves to protect and heal from situations that otherwise would create division and endless disputes. The resulting joy benefits us all because participating in the restoration of another generates gratitude which has us appreciating each other. In other words, be kind.

Research shows that kindness reduces stress and is a prosocial factor enhancing people's wellbeing. The abstract from an analytical review by David A Fryburg, MD gives concise insight into the effect of kindness.

He states:

> *"Chronic stress is a ubiquitous problem shouldered by many people worldwide. Although the stressors are myriad (eg, loneliness, finances, health, discrimination), the corporal response to them either causes or exacerbates mental and physical illness, including depression, anxiety, and cardiovascular disease. Identifying efficient ways to help people buffer their response and promote resilience and wellness is critical to improving overall health. Positive interpersonal connection is a proven way to promote resilience and happiness. It is associated with decreased mortality and markers of better health. Kindness and caring are prosocial behaviours that build positive interpersonal connections and can uplift both the giver and receiver. Simply seeing kindness and caring activates the neuropsychology of kindness, elevating the viewer and promoting generosity, interpersonal connection, and inclusion. That augmenting positive*

emotions, enhancing interpersonal
connection, and inducing prosocial
behaviour change are possible through
seeing kindness opens the opportunity
to bolster resilience in higher stress
settings like health care. In a recent
study, watching kindness media in a
health care setting rapidly increased
self-reported feelings of happiness,
calm, gratitude, and being inspired.
Viewers were significantly more
generous. Providing staff and patients
with a nonjudgmental lift to enhance
caring interactions through kindnesses
media can be an important, low-cost
adjunct to improving the healthcare
environment.[33]

There are many practical actions we can take to bring about immediate change. Local Municipalities can avail land for communities to grow fruit and vegetables. The whole operation can be supported from local government resources as a discharge of their duty to prioritise the needs of a community with food insecurity.

A farm can be built and managed by the municipality, of which the community manages it where cows and chickens could be herded for the production of milk, butter and cheese. Chickens produce eggs. This can go to feed the community at no cost to the community other than applying themselves in organised labour to tend to the farm, harvesting and distributing to everyone. This is a small example of how

---

[33] American Journal of Lifestyle Medicine, vol.16, no.1

changes to food insecurity can be dealt with. The use of genetically modified seeds must be avoided, because these produce crops from which the seeds cannot reproduce. These seeds are the design of corporate greed advanced by people such as Bill Gates and other corporations who use their vast money wealth to control farming. The effects of their intervention only serve their profit narrative that people should repeated buy seeds from them and thus depriving people of natural untempered food.

A pumpkin, for example, produces many seeds with can go to be planted and produce even more pumpkins, which means the community can't run out of such food.

The transport industry can offer free vehicles to communities for the purpose of transporting food. The industries are made of natural people themselves —people who need to eat and drink.

Housing can be provided for everyone. The resources all come from the earth and are processed with machinery that already exist. There is no need to restrict these resources when we apply them for the benefit people's needs.

The only real barrier to effecting the immediate changes is ourselves.

Anyone lacking the belief or will to pursue the works of neighbourly love and care for defining every aspect of our human activities, is overwhelmed with the courage of the uncourageous.

End.

www.ingramcontent.com/pod-product-compliance
Lightning Source LLC
Chambersburg PA
CBHW031130020426
42333CB00012B/313